ALL THE LEAVINGS

ALL THE LEAVINGS

LAURIE EASTER

Oregon State University Press   Corvallis

Cataloging-in-publication data is available from the Library of Congress.

♾ This paper meets the requirements of ANSI/NISO Z39.48-1992 (Permanence of Paper).

Oregon State University
OSU Press

Oregon State University Press
121 The Valley Library
Corvallis OR 97331-4501
541-737-3166 • fax 541-737-3170
www.osupress.oregonstate.edu

for Mary

and for June, John, Terri, and Christy

and finally

for Steve

The dry leaves . . . Do they fly or fall? Or does every flight contain the waiting earth? And does every fall contain the quiver of a wing?

—Dulce Maria Loynaz

CONTENTS

AUTHOR'S NOTE

This is a work of creative nonfiction. I have relied on memory, personal notes and records, and research when appropriate. In the interest of protecting privacy, a few names and identifying details have been changed.

PROLOGUE

Three hours into my drive from the home I was leaving in Forest Knolls, California, to the new one I had yet to make in southern Oregon, I heard a loud pop as one of the rear tires burst. The car tilted in a drag that slowed its momentum. I pulled onto the shoulder of Interstate 5, a corridor heavily populated by semitrucks running from Mexico to Canada. Here, in the northernmost section of the central valley of California, late in the afternoon on the Fourth of July, 1989, the sun cast its incessant ninety-five-degree heat on the agricultural fields of rice, wheat, and almonds. I did not have air conditioning, and the wind blew stifling air through the partially opened windows of the car. I could not unroll the windows further because my cat, Lacey, roamed the back seat untethered. Every Mack truck that whizzed by shook the vehicle. It smelled of dust and dry heat. Lacey began to meow.

I was twenty-three years old, five-and-a-half-months pregnant, traveling three hundred miles to meet my boyfriend in Mount Shasta. I had no cell phone (they wouldn't become popular for another ten years) and no money except for the fifty bucks my mother had given me "just in case." I had never changed a tire. I had no doubt I could do it under normal circumstances. But before I left the house in Forest Knolls, Margit, my soon-to-be ex-housemate, had helped me load my mountain bike into the trunk, where I assumed the spare lived. With my pregnant belly, it was too awkward for me to lift the bike out of the trunk.

I stepped out of the car that belonged to Steve, who had left for Oregon a week prior to caretake the land where we were going to live in a plywood hut with an earthen floor and one vinyl window on the other side of a creek with no bridge—a temporary situation until we figured out how and where to make a life for ourselves and our coming child. He had driven my truck to haul the bulk of our belongings. I drove his BMW 2002, which he had gotten cheap, fixed up, and spray-painted a dull, matte white.

It was around 5:30, and the highway was busy, with traffic speeding past. I opened the trunk and peered in, lifting the bike as best I could to search for the spare. I didn't see anything resembling a tire, so I got down on my hands and knees, gravel poking into my skin, and looked underneath the car. On my truck, that's where the spare lived, so I was hopeful. Nothing. I stood and glanced up and down the interstate. There was no exit in sight. The last town I had passed was Williams, California, about fifteen miles south. The irony was that our final destination was the town of Williams, Oregon. Right name. Wrong state.

I got back in the car and talked to Lacey, who was pacing around. She knew we were in trouble. So did I. *How could there not be a spare?* I wondered. Steve was a mechanic. He wouldn't send me off in a vehicle with no spare, would he? How was I going to get help when I had no way to make a call?

Finally, a man pulled over. He came to the passenger window.

"Do you need help changing your tire?" he asked.

"I don't have a spare," I said, lamely. *Who travels without a spare?!*

"Do you have towing service?"

"Yes, I have AAA."

"I'll call them at the next exit. In the meantime, put your hood up. It will alert a highway patrol that you're needing help."

I thanked the man. *It won't be long now,* I thought. Help was on the way. I opened the hood as he suggested and settled back into the driver's seat for the wait. The minutes, like the miles, stretched in a long, unending stream of cars zooming past. I sat, waiting, petting my cat, wondering how I was going to let Steve know I'd be late, dismayed that there was no spare tire, apprehensive at my circumstances.

Steve and I had been in a committed relationship for two years. We had spent the past ten months living together in a tiny three-bedroom house with four other adults and one young child. Each of us paid $85 a month rent. I worked as a housekeeper at a bed and breakfast inn and delivered pizzas for Domino's at night. Before that, I had roamed in my truck for a couple of months when Lacey was a kitten, staying here and there, not sure what I was doing or where I was going. I had moved out of the house where I'd lived for two years in Santa Cruz because I got a *feeling* it was time to go. That was how I made decisions. I trusted my intuition. If my gut told me it was time to leave, even if there was no plan for the future, I went with it. I had an innate trust that things would work out. Uncertainty seldom scared me.

Steve was thirteen years older and had spent many years on the road, living a gypsy life, working at his friend Larry's auto shop for weeks at a time to make enough money to last him months before going back to do it again. We were well matched in our desire for adventure, our willingness to take risks in achieving it, and our love for the natural world. When I got pregnant, we agreed to raise our child in the country. While Forest Knolls was close to the beauty of Point Reyes National Seashore, it was a bit like suburbia in the woods, populated by rich folks with whom we had no connection. Steve dreamed of raising a family in a place with strong community and an alternative lifestyle. He had lived communally, off-grid in his early twenties. The year prior, I'd fantasized about moving to a remote community I visited in the wilds of Northern California that required hiking several miles and wading across a river to access. The myth of such a life allured me. I was primed and ready. A conflict with one of our housemates in Forest Knolls solidified our decision to leave, and we decided on the small, rural town of Williams, a place populated by people committed to the adage *live and let live*, people who challenged mainstream notions and grounded themselves to the earth via farming and family. We knew a few people in the community, and the alternative elementary school enticed us.

In the car on the interstate, I sat waiting and waiting. Daylight waned as the sun settled below the distant, green mountains of the Mendocino National Forest to the west. At least now I felt relief from the heat. The sky turned dark. I wanted to turn on the hazard lights. But I didn't know how. I had never felt so ill equipped. I sat for more than four hours. One other person stopped not long after the first, and I told him someone had already called a tow truck. But had he? Highway patrol never came. How was it that not a single CHP officer drove by in four-hours' time?

Just as I was beginning to think I would be there all night, bright headlights shone in my rearview mirror. The tow truck driver said he was sorry, but being the Fourth of July, they were especially busy towing impounded vehicles from drivers under the influence. I climbed into his cab, holding Lacey in my arms. He asked if I wanted to go back to Williams or head north to Willows; it was about the same distance either way. I wanted to go to Willows. There was no sense in going backward, but I only had the $50 my mom gave me, and I needed a cheap motel. He said I could stay for free at the office of the towing company in Williams if I wanted. There was a couch I could sleep on, but the lights weren't working; I'd be there in total darkness.

So I went backward rather than forward into my new life. I wasn't making it to Shasta to meet Steve, and I wasn't making it to Oregon. But I could pretend because I would be in a town called Williams, even if there were 279 miles and more than a world of difference between the two. I opted for Motel 6 instead of the towing office. Once in my room, Lacey settled with food, water, and litterbox, I called my parents collect.

"I need you to do something," I told my dad. "I need you to call the police in Mount Shasta and give them the description of the motel where I'm supposed to meet Steve. I don't know the name, only what it looks like and how to get there because we've stayed there once before. I need them to find Steve and give him this number."

I was feeling better now that I wasn't sitting on the shoulder of I-5. My ingenuity was returning. I may not have been able to change the tire, and I may not have known how to turn on the hazard lights, but I could figure out a way to track down Steve.

Awhile later—an hour, maybe two?—the phone rang, and I heard Steve's voice.

"What happened?" he asked. "There was a knock on the door, and I thought it was you, but it turned out to be a cop. My heart sank, and I thought, *please don't give me bad news.*"

"I got a flat and there's no spare."

"There's a spare in the trunk."

"No, there's not. I looked."

"You have to lift up the floor panel," he said. "It's underneath."

This was too much for me—to learn there was a spare the whole time and I could have mustered the strength to find it or at least to have gotten the man who stopped to help me. If I had known or persisted in looking further, I would not have sat on the highway for four hours and would have already made it to Shasta. I would have solved my own problem instead of being dependent on others; something I hated. I burst into tears and cried, "I need you to come save me!"

I acted like the damn damsel in distress, the exact opposite of everything I always endeavored to be. I'd like to blame it on the pregnancy hormones. Incubating a tiny human assured my vulnerability and qualified my neediness. But perhaps there was more to it than that. Perhaps it was an indication I really didn't know what I was getting myself into. Perhaps making the life-altering decision to move to a new town in a new state, mid-pregnancy and with no money, and live in an earthen-floor hut with no water or electricity wasn't so much a sign of being a free spirit with an exorbitant amount of faith and ruggedness as it was an indication of being young, naïve, and ill-prepared. I didn't know what it meant to be a mother, how it would challenge me in ways I could never predict and far worse than getting a flat on the highway. I didn't know anything about off-grid living. I had done a lot of camping, even two separate month-long backpacking trips as a teenager, one in the backcountry of the high Sierras and one in Death Valley. I had exhibited strength and grit and the capacity to survive difficult situations. But at twenty-three years old, I embarked on motherhood without much forethought or planning.

Without complaint, Steve abandoned the already-paid-for motel room in Shasta and made the two-and-a-half-hour drive south. In the morning, we went to the dusty lot where the car sat alone, looking forlorn, tilted on its axis. Steve opened the trunk, unloaded my bike and other stored items, and pulled out the spare. I felt only relief at the ease in which he changed the tire and comfort at his willingness to come help me.

We headed north, leaving behind our past, driving straight up the interstate into a precarious future, one full of hope. I didn't know yet that to give birth to joy means also giving rise to heartache—that love and loss are mirror faces reflecting one another.

HER BODY, A WILDERNESS

My second daughter was born on the plywood living-room floor between the woodstove and bathtub—naturally, like a bear cub born in a den. However, our den, on the fringe of wilderness, had hot running water and lights, thanks to an on-demand propane water heater and solar electricity. Only weeks before her birth, we had expanded our rustic one-room cabin with a separate bedroom and loft. The new bedroom overlooked golden yarrow, black-eyed Susan, purple coneflower, sweet William—and the lawn, meadow, and encircling forest. Still, with all that beauty to envelop her, Akela was not ready to experience the wildness. She preferred the warmth and safety of the womb and seemed quite content to stay there.

Two weeks past my due date, Ruth, my midwife, recommended I take castor oil to induce labor, so I blended vanilla ice cream and root beer with a four-ounce bottle of castor oil.

"The carbonation and ice cream will cut the heaviness of the oil," Ruth had said.

And she was right. I drank the shake quickly, before the ingredients had time to separate. It was a brilliant, sunny afternoon, the first day of autumn, and the yellow light shone into the kitchen where I sat at the table looking out the window at the pine and fir trees.

A friend knocked on the door unexpectedly just as I was downing the drink. I lifted the glass to her. "Cheers!" I said. "Here's to going into labor."

Afterward, I lay my cumbersome belly down on its side in the shade of the grass and promptly fell asleep. When I awoke a couple hours later, my bowels screamed to let loose. The castor oil had done its job, lubricating my insides and inducing my body to expel everything within. After several trips to the outhouse, my stomach began to contract, tight and thunderous, in intervals a minute apart. I'd barely catch my breath from a contraction before the roll of the next. Labor was off and running like a logging truck with no brakes sliding down the mountain. The sun set, and wind began to blow in and around the trees, swirling through leaves and pine needles, singing in long, slow breaths that whistled and roared. In a white, button-down shift, I walked barefoot in the cool grass, hands on my belly, groaning with the wind.

Steve scoured the footless claw-foot bathtub until the faded white enamel coating of the cast iron shined. I lowered myself into the warm water and lay submerged on my side. After a time, I felt a sudden expansive pop, an explosion that burst within my insides. Iridescent flecks of amniotic fluid floated over the surface of the bath water, pearlescent and glittering. Then I had to vomit. I got out of the tub, sat on a stool, and heaved into a metal bowl.

The baby was coming fast now. With Steve on one side of me and my friend Hollis on the other to hold me in a squat, I began to push. But when her head emerged, the baby tried to take a breath while the rest of her body remained inside, lungs compressed, and her anterior shoulder was caught underneath my pubic bone.

"Get on your hands and knees," Ruth instructed. I got on all fours, mama-bear style, and with deft hands, Ruth reached in to loosen the baby's shoulder from its obstruction. "Push. Now!" she ordered.

Five and a half hours after contractions began, Akela's body slipped out, the umbilical cord wrapped tightly around her neck twice. She lay cradled in Ruth's hands, limp, gray, and unresponsive, an Apgar score of one out of ten. A total Apgar score of three or below requires immediate resuscitation. Akela scored a one because she had a heartbeat. But it was low and getting lower. Ruth unwound the cord and gently jostled her tiny, wet body to encourage a response, but as the seconds ticked by, Akela did not breathe. Ruth gave her mouth to mouth. Two little puffs. Akela's body brightened with a pink hue just like a desert sunrise spreading from horizon toward the fading stars. She cried then, forced to accept her place in the world.

With all the attention focused on the baby, nobody noticed the blood squirting out of me in sudden forceful streams. "Am I supposed to be bleeding this much?" I asked.

"No," Ruth said. She reached into her bag, pulled out a syringe, and prepared it with a dose of Pitocin. "Turn over," she instructed. She jabbed the needle into the flesh of my ass. My uterus began to contract. The bleeding slowed, then stopped. They handed me the baby.

For the first week, her eyes were vague as I held her. It felt like her spirit hovered outside her body, caught between the worlds. But it was a strong spirit. I could feel it.

At twelve years old, Akela was muscular, strong, fierce. A gymnast, she pushed her body past comfort and tolerated pain in the process of attaining perfection. Hard workouts exhilarated her—the ache of fifty push-ups, the soreness of two hundred crunches, the burn of leg lunges across four lengths of gym floor. She relished testing her capabilities and moving beyond the realm of standard expectation. She was competitive—not only with others, but with herself.

Unlike her older sister Lily and me, who complain about any bump or scrape, Akela has a high threshold to pain and tends not to say when she is hurting but, instead, becomes quiet and withdraws. There have been exceptions, like the time she wiped out on her bicycle while riding down our gravel driveway, which meanders between oak trees. She got to the curve in the road before gliding down into the meadow, but the tires skidded on the loose rocks, sending her crashing into them bare-legged. She got a gash on her knee that left a scar. She cried then—wailed in fact. She must have been five or six. There was also the time she picked up a young garter snake slithering through the lawn (she commonly handled critters: snakes, frogs, praying mantises). The snake bit her on the thumb and wouldn't let go. Akela stood with her arm outstretched, trying to shake the snake loose, but it held on, its tiny jaw clamped tight. Akela screamed, although her bulging eyes, pleading with me to rid her hand of its new writhing appendage, told me she suffered more from terror than pain. She was nine.

My children were raised in the country most of their childhoods, on twenty-eight acres of forested hillside, with a sloping meadow and pockets of clearings nestled among firs and cedars, a smattering of pines, solid oaks, and madrone trees with ruddy, peeling bark. Years before we bought the land, it had been selectively logged, but the remaining trees flourished, creating a healthy forest that nurtured ferns, wild irises, and ceanothus; foxes, skunks, and raccoons; owls, pileated woodpeckers, deer, and cougar. The land sits on the north side of Grayback Mountain, nestled just below Little Sugarloaf peak in the Siskiyou Mountains, five miles as the hawk glides from Oregon Caves National Monument. Driving up the road past our driveway, one would continue climbing steeply up the mountain into old-growth forest and, unfortunately, more and more clear-cuts. Often, I would take this drive, alone or with the girls and our dog, to walk on empty forest service roads, looking down on the valley and soaking in the quiet. There is a stillness up there on the mountain, the only sounds a rustling breeze, the murmur of a distant creek, the flapping wings of a surprised pheasant—or the crunching of my own footfall.

To the west some twenty miles rests the 179,755-acre Kalmiopsis Wilderness, designated by Congress in 1964 and named for the rare, pre–ice age flowering plant *Kalmiopsis leachiana*, discovered by Lilla Leech in 1930. The Kalmiopsis Wilderness, renowned for its plant diversity, unique geology, and wild sections of the Illinois, Chetco, and North Fork Smith Rivers, boasts an expanse of coveted roadless old-growth forest. That is, it did until 2002 when lightning caused the Biscuit Fire—the largest fire in North America that year—to rage nearly 500,000 acres, including all of the Kalmiopsis. During that summer we mostly stayed inside, for the smoke was so dense we could smell it from within the house even with the doors and windows closed. Smoke seeped through the cracks of our unsealed cabin, a mild stench of burn permeating the walls. It was mid-July and difficult to stay indoors, but the alternative—to go out—was more unpleasant. At times, the smoke was so thick you could barely see the trees in the forest, like driving through fog and not knowing when a deer might be standing in the road ahead, only this fog was brown-tinged and roasted.

It took five and a half months to fully contain the Biscuit Fire. As its primary fire suppression strategy, the US Forest Service intentionally set back-burns (some of which grew out of control), which eventually constituted between a third and half of the total area of the fire. Seventy-five percent of vegetation was killed, including thousands of old-growth trees, and much wildlife habitat was lost. It pained me to think of all those hundreds-of-years-old conical spires burning to a crisp and the birds and animals fleeing in fright—despite my belief that fire is part of the natural process, an essential ecological step in long-term forest health. Nature, I believed, was meant to be left to its own design, a domain independent from humans, not to be tampered with. Although wilderness turns on itself, it also has an incredible capacity to heal itself. A forest may burn uncontrollably, but with time, new seedlings sprout, regenerating the damaged ecosystem, as evidenced in the Kalmiopsis: pine trees have sprouted under the protection of the burned timber stand and many plants continue to thrive. Still, after the fire, a years-long battle ensued in the courts over the salvage timber sale. Some wanted to harvest the standing dead timber and replant. Others, like me, wanted the wilderness to be left to its own natural process of recovery.

I once heard someone say he considered his body a wilderness. Wildness lives in our external environment, functioning independently and without the aid of humans. Complex, integrated ecosystems work to support each other and maintain balance. Similarly, within our bodies a myriad of functions occurs simultaneously without conscious thought. We walk through life—or run or skip or trudge—and most often we never question how our bodies operate, hour after hour, day after day, year after year—until something malfunctions and we are forced to acknowledge our fragility. We take our bodies for granted much the way we have come to take for granted fresh water, clean air, nutritious food.

❂

Five years after the Biscuit Fire, when we had relocated to town for a time so the girls could attend public school, Akela came home from dinner out with a friend at a local pizza parlor and said, "My stomach hurts." She went straight to bed. Only a couple days earlier she had recovered from the flu, and I worried that I had let her go out too soon and she might be having a relapse. She slept till noon the next day. When she awoke, she continued to complain about her stomach and began to vomit. Her temperature rose to 101 degrees. Because a stomach flu was circulating the community, I felt certain that with her immunity down, she had fallen victim. I called the emergency room, describing her symptoms, only to have a nurse confirm my speculation.

But the nurse and I were wrong.

Her body was no longer a pristine mountain to be weathered by time but an erupting volcano. The small opening between her appendix and her colon became blocked, causing increased pressure and inflammation until her appendix perforated, sending a profusion of bacteria-laced fluids into her abdomen and bloodstream. But we didn't know it had happened until two days later when we rushed her to the emergency room, her hands and feet cold, her skin sallow, her temperature ninety-four degrees.

The CT scan showed an abnormal amount of fluid in her abdomen, evidence that something had ruptured. But due to the excess of fluid, the doctors could not determine what. Her liver and kidneys were barely functioning. Even though I'd been encouraging her to drink lots of water, she was completely dehydrated. All the water proved futile. More fluids leaked into her abdomen than she was able to ingest to hydrate her organs. The surgeon said they would need to do exploratory surgery, but when he tried to pull together a team, no one would back him. Her condition was too critical, and they were not versed in pediatrics. Akela was transported by Mercy Flights to Doernbecher Children's Hospital at Oregon Health Sciences University in Portland.

There was room for only one of us to fly with Akela. Accompanying her terrified me. I feared I would have a complete emotional breakdown and be a burden rather than support, so when Steve insisted on going with her, I did not argue and arranged passage on a commercial plane. It was nearing the end of the day, and there was only one remaining flight to Portland. I had to pack, make sure Lily was cared for, and then drive twenty miles to the airport, all within an hour. My adrenaline kicked in. The possibility of missing that plane and being five hours later arriving at OHSU—the time it would take to drive—was so emotionally debilitating I could not bear to give it a second thought. But it was there, needling me, whispering my worst fear: if I don't get there in time and Akela doesn't survive, *I* will never survive.

As I drove, with my mother silent in the passenger seat, I focused all my attention on getting there, not missing that flight. I veered my Subaru around cars, zooming back and forth between semis and other vehicles. Occasionally I glanced in the rearview mirror, but mostly my eyes were directed forward, concentrating on what lay ahead. I was so focused I did not notice passing Grizzly Peak or the brown, snow-topped hills enveloping the Rogue Valley or the horses in their pastures along the highway. I did not notice that the sun was setting or that the temperature was dropping. I was oblivious to the revving of the car's engine and the whooshing of the wind as it collided with my window. I did not notice as my car passed through Talent into Phoenix and on into Medford that all around me life was carrying on, just like any other day, people leaving work, going shopping, driving home.

Over the phone the travel agent had said, "You must arrive at least half an hour early to get your ticket, or the counter will be closed." I arrived fifteen minutes late, and although the counter was still open, I was prepared to defend my territory on that plane if I were denied access. Nothing was going to prevent me from getting to my daughter. Nothing.

Boarding pass in hand, I took off my shoes, passed through security, and joined the group waiting for the flight to Portland. Within two minutes, the gate opened for boarding. Normally I get sick on airplanes and have mild anxiety. But there was no room for that on this flight. I just sat, numb yet terrified. Steve and Akela had already boarded the Mercy Flights plane and awaited takeoff. As my aircraft departed, Steve watched, telling a nearly unconscious Akela, "There goes your mom."

When I arrived at the pediatric intensive care unit, Akela lay there, hooked to monitors and intravenous fluids, a swarm of doctors and nurses gathered around her. They asked me endless questions and offered possible scenarios of diagnosis while preparing to do exploratory surgery. Amidst all this activity, one thing I wasn't aware of was that my body kept functioning. My heart kept pumping blood. My lungs kept taking in oxygen. My brain kept sending messages to neurons. In that moment, I never questioned how my body knew exactly what to do. All I questioned was whether my daughter would recover, whether her body was strong enough to fight off the infection, whether it was too late.

❁

We had been home barely twenty-four hours when Akela spiked a fever of 101 degrees and had to be taken to the emergency room. She had been released from OHSU two days earlier, appearing to be healthy and on the mend, after spending eight days recovering from surgery. Dr. Harrison, her surgeon, had warned us of the possibility she might develop an abscess.

"If she gets a fever, take her to the hospital immediately," he had said. "She will need to have it drained."

Unbelievable.

Another round of doctors and nurses. Another batch of gut-wrenching contrast material she had to drink on an empty stomach. Another CT scan. *Why hadn't they kept her at OHSU another day?* She appeared to be healing. *Why didn't they do a CT scan to make sure she was okay before releasing her?* That is not how CT scans are used: they are expensive and expose the body to excessive amounts of radiation.

It was a sleepy Sunday night around ten o'clock when we took her into our local emergency room. Akela was the only patient in the ER, yet they still didn't quite know what to do with her. They performed a CT scan, and believing her not to be in immediate danger, admitted her to the hospital, put her on an IV with lactated ringers and full-spectrum antibiotics, and placed her in a room at the end of the hall of the original wing of the hospital, an old room with low particle-board ceilings, unused equipment, two hospital beds, a chair that folded out into a makeshift bed, and a window that overlooked the parking lot but was covered in heavy drapery.

Late the next afternoon, the surgeon entered the room and introduced himself. As he looked down his nose at me, I got the distinct feeling his downward gaze had little to do with my shortness of height. There was no handshake, very few questions. My stomach tightened. I was the only parent present.

"She has two abscesses," he said. "They need to be drained. I'll go in through her back and drain them through a tube inserted in her rectum. It's a simple procedure." This doctor didn't mess around. He was all business, straight to the point. Then he said, "If I had been on duty when she came in the first time, I could have done the surgery. It would have been a very simple operation. There really was no reason for her to be sent to Portland. The people on duty didn't know what they were doing."

The people on duty didn't know what they were doing?

They erred on the side of caution, acknowledging the fact that operating on a twelve-year-old is different from operating on an adult. They realized their limitations and, assessing her condition, made the best possible decision, which was to send her to a pediatric hospital. They did not want to risk losing her on account of their egos. This man had never seen Akela. He didn't even look at her now. He had only diagnosed her CT scan and read her chart, and I doubted he had given it more than a glance. I wonder if he saw her as a commodity, like the trees in the Kalmiopsis: harvest them and add an extra ten grand to the bank account. Doctors like this were part of the reason I avoided traditional medicine. My jaw and neck tensed. I gritted my teeth. If I were a wolf, my hackles would have stood on end. "She was very ill," I said. "She had sepsis, and her organs were shutting down."

"All she needed was to be operated on and cleaned out. I could have done it." This repeated assertion of his competence—not to mention the incompetence of his colleagues—and disregard for the seriousness of Akela's condition grated me like a bulldozer scraping granite. "It really was no big deal. Appendicitis happens all the time. She probably wasn't even in the ICU." This last part was an assumption, not a question.

No big deal. My kid just had kidney and liver failure. Her blood was saturated with bacteria.

"She was in the ICU for two days," I said. "She nearly died."

He left without speaking to Akela.

When he came back, Steve was present. The surgeon approached Akela. No introduction as to who he was. No "How are you doing?" He sat on her bed, his weight lowering the side of the mattress, torqueing her spine and buckling her stomach, like earth during a quake.

"Ow, get off the bed, get off the bed," she cried in pain.

He continued to sit and just stared at her.

"Get off the bed, it hurts."

Steve and I exchanged deliberate glances. We were not only on the same page, but we were at the very same paragraph, the very same sentence, which read: This is not going to work; we've got to find an alternative.

With what little energy she had, Akela yelled, "Get off the bed!" She glared.

Casually, slowly, he rose. "This is how it's going to work," he said to her. "I'm going to get your abscesses taken care of. I'm going to try to do it in the least invasive way possible. But I may have to cut you open again and go in through your original incision."

"I don't want to be cut open again. I don't want another surgery," she said, tears surfacing. The stress of the last ten days was winning the struggle. When the surgeon left the room, she said, "I hate him."

The doctor on duty and several nurses told us that this man did not have a good bedside manner, but he was an excellent surgeon—the best. Whether this was true or he simply believed it, his actions left us convinced there was no way that man was going to touch our daughter. His demeanor did not nurture trust but rather a belief that overzealous confidence could lead to fallibility. It was eight o'clock at night and snow was beginning to weigh down tree branches and turn the roads white. Still, Steve called Dr. Harrison and explained the situation—that we didn't like the surgeon, that we felt safer with him, Dr. Harrison, that this hospital really wasn't conducive to children the way Doernbecher was.

"You're welcome to come back up here," Dr. Harrison said. "I don't know if we can do it any better than they can there, but you can bring her back. We'd be happy to see her."

So here we were at Doernbecher once again, preparing for surgery number two to drain both abscesses, one the size of a grapefruit adhered to her uterus, the other stuck to her bladder. Reddish-purple, bluish-black, greenish-yellow. Those were the colors of Akela's arms. The patches melded into each other, different stages of bruising progression, holes from needle pricks dotted throughout. Her veins had had enough. They were barely visible, receding the way the tide sucks a wave back to the ocean. Struggling to find a suitable spot to insert an IV, the nurses called in a specialist from the PICU. She scanned both Akela's arms and hands, settling with a vein on her wrist. She rubbed antiseptic on it, prepared the syringe, and in one smooth shot IV number fourteen slid into place.

For the next five days straight, I confined myself within the hospital walls, keeping vigil at Akela's bedside. The wilderness of her body raged from the volcanic eruption of a ruptured appendix, the spreading fire of sepsis and ensuing dehydration, the threatened ecosystem of mild kidney and liver failure, the firefighter response of exploratory abdominal surgery, the natural complication of abscesses, and the backup team's implementation of a second surgery, which left her with two tubes sticking out of her belly—all within a span of two weeks. Steve and I watched as she withered away into near nothingness, skin on bones and a wounded, fragile spirit. There is only so much a parent can take before cracking from mental and emotional stress. I was at breaking point. I had to get out. My sanity demanded it. So while Akela lay napping, I slipped from her room.

I escaped out the grand hospital entrance—high ceiling, tiled floor, and circular driveway—through the parking lot, up an outdoor stairway, and onto the street. The season had been transforming from winter to spring without my knowing. Daffodils were blooming, and narcissus and crocus—bright spots of color in a crisp and bare landscape of pavement-lined yards and leafless trees. I swept around the U-shaped road, past buildings labeled "School of Nursing" and "Campus Services," then followed a side road that bent around to the entrance of the Veterans Hospital. I needed earth: dirt, plants, trees. A winding foot path beckoned me across the street.

The beginning of the path was lined with planted trees and roses. Each had a plaque, a memorial marker designating for whom that tree or rose had been planted. Some had been hospital employees, others patients—all people gone from the physical world, all people loved and honored. "Memorial Lane," I called it as I passed the dedicated quotations. *How sad to lose someone you love.* I hurried along, fearful to linger.

The path was not long, not hidden or private, yet it conjured the feeling of escape. Winding snakelike among dense firs and rhododendron, the path offered solitude, relief, perspective. Along its edges there were two benches—the type found in English gardens, wrought iron framing with a wooden seat. I chose the bench surrounded by plant life, where sunshine filtered through openness at the end of the path, creeping stealthily among the shadows. It was the farthest from any buildings, the farthest from civilization, the farthest from my current reality. The bench was cold. Sunshine streamed on my face. I closed my eyes and breathed fresh outdoor air, not the recycled filtered air of the hospital. Sturdy, rooted, age-old beings towered over me, protecting me, gathering me in their embrace, if only for a moment.

Few instants in life a person finds herself wrapped fully in the present, ensconced in the crystalline now, every particle of her being, every atom of her molecular structure poised in the experience. These rare moments, fleeting glimpses of true presentness, tend to surface during extreme tribulations. And there in my miniforest, I found myself existing within timelessness: sitting, watching, breathing. I had caught the last minutes of afternoon sun and stolen peacefulness. When the light finally faded beyond my reach and responsibility weighed on me, the delicate thread connecting me to my daughter gave a gentle tug and called me back, away from the grounded trees, away from the sword ferns, back to the inside world of pain, illness, and prayer.

❂

Three months after the surgeries, my twelve-year-old daughter wears a battle scar: a five-inch-long, half-inch-wide, raw, reddish-purple welt running vertically down her abdomen. The scar has horizontal ridges, as though the gaping cavity had been merely zipped back together. On each side are two smaller scars a few inches out from the center and low, just above her bikini line, where tubes drained her two abscesses. They appear like the dimples on her cheeks, only one of them sticks out while the other goes in. I told her they would fade. They would not always stand as blazing announcements declaring her survival. Still, I was not certain.

My eyes gravitated toward the middle scar, a mark so large and unexpected on the stomach of a child, as if my vision were the negatively charged end of a magnet drawn to her positively charged abdomen. The doctors told us she should wear a one-piece bathing suit so the sun wouldn't darken the scar. Akela resisted this—she is a bikini girl through and through—yet she cooperated, knowing the importance of the healing process for "fitting in" and appearing to be a "normal kid." But her time of normalcy had passed. A young girl does not fight such a battle and remain the same. Some moments she did not seem to care if the scars were noticeable. She almost seemed proud, as if they symbolized a major accomplishment. And they do.

"I know why it happened to me," she said once she was recovering back at home. "Because I was strong enough to survive it."

"Yes," I said. "You are right. You are very strong."

There is a whole universe inside our bodies, a wild, untamed universe. Humans have tried to conquer the wilderness of outdoor nature, to wield it to serve and benefit our own desires. Similarly, we have tried to conquer our inner wilderness by manipulating and controlling disease and pain within our human shells. Akela had become septic. Bacteria multiplied in a pus-filled environment and spread throughout her bloodstream, attacking every "normal" function of her body. Her inner wilderness was ablaze with a fire of catastrophic proportions, a fire out of control, consuming everything in its path. Her only chance at survival was the human urge to conquer and control the uncontrollable. They cut her open and hosed out her insides, sprayed and sprayed at the fire, attempting to extinguish it or at least to smolder it. Then they hooked her to a successive drip of three types of broad-spectrum intravenous antibiotics: a human creation designed not only to control but obliterate bacteria. And the process persisted. Oxygen was added to her intake of breath. Bile was pumped out of her stomach through a tube in her nose. Morphine dripped into her veins to manage the pain. Bolus after bolus of lactated ringers, sodium chloride, and potassium chloride supplemented her system. And ever so slowly, her wilderness recovered, not by any natural process of recovery, but by the commitment to dominate, subdue, and manage that wilderness.

Three and a half months after the onset of her appendicitis, Akela's gymnastics team had an end-of-year celebration and performance. Akela had returned to workouts barely four weeks earlier, starting slowly, no tumbling, nothing but stretching and strength building. She hadn't gained much weight back. Her leotard and gym shorts hung baggy and loose; there was no muscle to grab onto, no curve to her butt, merely a straight slope from her back toward her feet. When she first returned, another girl's mom, a nurse, was concerned and consulted the coach. The word *anorexia* may have been mentioned. This surprised me because at that point she looked much improved from what she had before. But I had the grisly memory of her depleted self. Anything looked healthy compared to that.

Girls flew through the air, swinging on bars, vaulting over mats, running and tumbling on the floor. Akela could do only a few things: back walkovers, handstand forward rolls, dance moves. She looked happy, back in her element, her wan face smiling, content to participate in the thing she loved. At the finale, Akela surprised us and did a standing back handspring. It was not perfect. But it was her. Doing it. Steve and I sat, overwhelmed, watching our daughter, her body, a wilderness that once needed intervention, now on the path to restoration.

Parents clapped and cheered their children. They were not thinking about the randomness of nature. They were not thinking about how one bolt of lightning can consume a forest.

RELICS

I call it the Death Box.

I lift it from where it rests atop a pine bedside cabinet, between a six-foot-high bookcase and a secondhand dresser missing its bottom drawer. The box feels solid in my hands and warm as its chestnut color. A fire-breathing sea serpent threatens from the carving etched into the lid and the front face, amidst swirling Van Gogh's *Starry Night* clouds and waves: guardian of the box. The sides and back are carved with flowers curling at the base of a vessel, its bottom round as a giant pumpkin with a removable lid. The corners of the box are notched together snug as jigsaw pieces. Two brass hinges connect the lid to the base, and it latches closed on the front with a tarnished brass clasp stamped with four star-shaped flowers.

I carry the box from the bedroom to the kitchen, smooth the tabletop to clear it of dust, and set the box down. Lifting the clasp, I lean the lid back until it stands perpendicular. A trove lies within the four-and-a-half-by-nine-inch walls. I have always been a collector, from the time I was a very young child. Revisiting relics from the past soothes me, so I reach inside and withdraw some of the contents, setting them on the table.

A heavy-duty brass lock in the shape of an antique carpenter's toolbox
Two cowrie shells
One thumbnail-sized nugget of polished auburn and banded gray agate
A carved mother of pearl hairpiece with dried pressed flowers and leaves
   beneath a shiny lacquered coating

A silver bell tied to a piece of dark green, twisted cord
A fortune cookie fortune: "People respond to your beautiful smile."

I pretend the box belonged to my Grandma June. But it didn't. It belonged to my mother, and my Great-Aunt Madge before her. This box is the twin to June's, which sat atop the antique desk in her den, next to the antique clock that now sits in my parents' living room. "Grandma June can't die. She has to live forever," I used to say emphatically, as if by stating this I could prevent the inevitable from happening. When the call notifying me of June's death came, I was watching Robert Redford and Meryl Streep picnicking on the African savannah. My mother's voice spoke words I did not wish to hear. And as Karen, the baroness and coffee plantation owner in *Out of Africa*, mourned the loss of her lover, Denys, from a plane crash, I was in my room crying over the loss of my Grandma June from an aortic aneurysm.

A key to a safety deposit box
A crisp $2 bill
One 2007 Sean Adams Golden Dollar
Nine Sacajawea Golden Dollar coins from the year 2000
One 2003 silver frosted uncirculated $1 Kangaroo Coin from the Royal
  Australian Mint
A copper-plated Queen Elizabeth Two Pence
A darkened 1945 wheat penny "One Cent"

Within days of June's death, Steve and I traveled south from Oregon with our children, ages six and one, for a small family gathering to scatter June's ashes. Steve played with the girls on Angel Island's beach as the rest of our family sailed on the San Francisco Bay in a rented boat to disperse June: dull, gray ash and ivory bone fragments into cold, gray-green water.

The day before we spread her ashes, my brothers and I sat on the maroon carpeting of our parents' living room, circling a few miscellaneous items that had belonged to June—stray pieces that neither my mother nor my aunt wanted. We were polite with one another as we divvied up who would get what. Mike wanted the box. I wanted the box too. But this was not a time for bickering over leftovers. So I remained quiet and nodded my acquiescence. I took what my brothers did not want:

A black, cast-iron Chinese teapot

A flat, palm-sized, three-quarter-inch-thick piece of polished petrified wood—
  smooth and rounded—mottled patches of ebony, coffee, and cream

A conical, spiraled mother of pearl shell that shimmers rainbow iridescence and
  whispers the ocean when held to the ear

A Washi box covered with handcrafted decorative Japanese paper

Had June gotten the teapot on her trip to China? The trip on which she brought photos of me, aged twelve, posing with her robust German shepherd, to show the Chinese people she met, whose eyes grew wide at seeing the dog's mass and smiled appreciatively that he would make good and plentiful eating. Had she brought the shell home from Indonesia or Burma or Thailand, found it in a beachside gift shop along the Bay of Bengal or the Java Sea? Had the petrified wood been in her possession since girlhood? Did she sit on her bed in the evenings and rub the cool smoothness with her fingertips the way the ancient Greeks rubbed worry stones?

Later that evening, after my brothers and I finished sorting through June's belongings, I confided to my mother my disappointment at not receiving the box.

She said, "I've got one just like it you can have. It belonged to Madge." June's long-dead younger sister.

I accepted the box graciously, never mentioning that its significance was diluted because it hadn't belonged to June. I placed Grandma June's shell and petrified wood inside—the Washi box and teapot would not fit.

One baby tooth and four loose eyelashes, belonging to one or the other of my
  children

A flat circular tuft of blue T-shirt fuzz tenderly plucked from Steve's belly button

One dull feline tooth

Twenty-one kitty whiskers, all white, three with black ends—the coarse ends
  once anchored in kitty muzzle

Whiskers. A whisker stuck in the carpet, a whisker on the down comforter, a whisker on the couch. Lacey and Minu whiskers. Lacey lived to be twenty, Minu a month shy of nineteen. Lacey used to sneak under the covers and sleep snuggled in the crook of my arm. Minu's fur was soft as an angora rabbit. Toward the end of their lives, whenever I'd find a stray whisker, I'd drop it into the box, jesting to myself that maybe I could clone them.

Now, I twirl them between my fingers, feel the stiff ends. I slide them to one side of the box, a gathering of whiskers, along with my children's eyelashes and the teeth. The blue fuzz I squish between fingertips, molding its round tuft further before tucking it into the corner with the rest.

Two handmade Christmas present tags cut from watercolor paper, folded and loosely painted with small flowers by Grandma June, given to me by my aunt
One page of three-by-five-inch lined paper torn from a notebook with ratty, frayed edge still attached to the left-hand side, on which is written in black pen in June's shaky script:

> *Lily's measurements*
> *9/20/91*
> *around neck 10 ½ inches*
> *neck (outer arm) to wrist 10 ½"*
> *underarm to wrist 7"*
> *to waist 4-5"*
> *waist 19"*
> *neck to waist 8"*
> *waist to ankle 16"*
> *leg (inseam) 10 ½*
>
> *neck to ankle 18"*
> *waist 24*
> *chest 24*
> *hip*

The relics remind me of a time fading into history, a time when people handwrote letters, when cursive was a necessary skill for speed and ease of communication, a time when "handmade" was not merely considered quaint but common. A time when Lily stood approximately two feet tall.

June's list of measurements crinkles between my fingers. I gaze at her unsteady scrawl, wobbly from chronic arthritis, so familiar, so knowable, yet no longer in existence except on this thin scrap of paper. Is handwriting like a fingerprint? A singular, identifiable trait, no two exactly alike?

Hair from Akela's first haircut, golden-blond wisps fine as corn silk tied into a ponytail with a gold metallic hair tie

A small piece of white tracing paper with tiny red hearts stamped all over that
reads in a young girl's hand: "I Love you mom Love Lily"
A folded piece of black paper with a mouth of white lips drawn in gel pen on
the front that opens to read in an even younger girl's hand: "I Love you so so
much I can't stand It Love Akela" with three green hearts at the bottom and
one pink heart at the top

I stroke the ponytail. Now, Akela's hair is russet brown and hangs in long, gentle waves down her back.

Two handmade valentines: red and pink construction paper hearts cut and
glued on top of each other in gradation and sprinkled with glitter, addressed
on the back "To Mom" and signed by each of the girls
A wallet-sized photo of seven-year-old Akela on one bent knee in the grass,
wearing shin guards, athletic shorts, and blue jersey, a red and white soccer
ball resting on her knee, a gap instead of two front teeth
A photo of me and nine-year-old Lily, sitting on my mother-in-law's couch.
Lily's legs rest on the couch, one on top of the other, sideways at an angle, a
blue-jean mermaid tail with feet. She leans into my side, a hand on my leg,
her head tilted back and toward mine, resting against my cheek. My arms are
wrapped round her waist, one palm flat on her stomach, the other palm flat
on her chest

My hair was thick and brown then, no dull luster of sandy sprinkles, no unruly frizz. My complexion was smooth, unlined, without the dark circles now beneath my eyes. No double chin. The tendons in my neck still showed. I could still wear my fitted, green rayon dress, the one hand-embroidered in India, size small. I was thirty-two.

A tarnished, sterling-silver puzzle ring: four bands interlocked with one another
hang loose—an unfinished puzzle—an empty stone-setting on one band,
where an oval turquoise cabochon is missing

My friend Liza made puzzle rings, silver and gold ornate labyrinths. Some had four, six, eight bands. They looked like Celtic knots that could be taken apart and reconfigured. At her craft fairs, Liza showed customers how to slide each singular band into place, folding and looping bands through and around one another until the pieces fit together. A puzzle maker, a puzzle teacher, fingering silver bands the way a yogi fingers mala beads, twirling, practicing, solving life's puzzles. There was one puzzle she did not solve, however, until it was too late: the malignant lump on her hip.

A delicate cotton handkerchief, the fabric so thin I can see through it. The center is a white square framed by tiny, yellow daffodil-like flowers, framed by larger pink roses, framed by a faded periwinkle, netting-like print with a scalloped edge in pink

A tiny, padded fuchsia-colored Chinese jewelry bag with bright yellow trim and snap

A miniature envelope with a card inside that reads:

> *23 February 2001*
> *Dear Laurie,*
> *These two rings belonged to my dear friend Pauline Adams. I'm sending them to you as a memento of the day many years ago that Peggy invited us to lunch and you made the muffins.*
> *Love Mary*

Marguerite, for whom I was a caregiver at the end of her eighty-five-year life, collected handkerchiefs. At her memorial, her daughters let me choose one to keep. I unfold the cloth and hold it up to the light, looking through the fabric to what lies beyond, like a veil between the worlds.

Inside the Chinese bag rest two rings wrapped in white tissue paper. One is a platinum lady's eternity band, a single band set with diamonds along its circumference, and the other a white-gold lady's Art Deco diamond ring with sapphires. I slide each ring onto one of my fingers. They feel awkward, bulky and displaced, so I take them off, rewrap them, and close them back inside the satin pouch.

Pauline was an old woman in Mary's life. Marguerite was an old woman in mine. How auspicious it was that Mary, my mother's best friend, would send these rings to me just after Marguerite died. When I thanked her, writing of the synchronicity, she responded, "The timing of the package certainly is interesting—it seems that more is going on in our lives than we know."

A water-stained photo printed on regular copy paper of a young woman with bulbous, hazel eyes; narrow brows arched like rainbows; thin, straight brown hair; long nose; pointy chin; and a soft, crooked smile: Cassie

Prior to leaving town, Cassie went on a vision quest, hosted a "Sister's Circle" on All Hallow's Eve in which she burned a coyote pelt as a symbolic act of release, gave away most of her possessions, and moved out of her house. During all her preparations, she would state, "I am going where Spirit takes me."

Cassie left, car packed with her remaining possessions, including wreaths she had made from dried flowers to give as gifts to her family, with whom she was going to be flying to Europe. She had only been traveling a couple of hours on the windy mountain road when she accidently veered onto the shoulder, overcorrected her steering, and lost control of her car. She was hit directly by an oncoming vehicle driven by a minister en route to his new church. He survived unscathed. The authorities told him that if not for the air bags in his brand-new car, he would have died alongside Cassie. At the crash site, dried flowers from Cassie's wreaths lay scattered across the highway.

The last time I spoke with Cassie she had called to invite me to the Halloween Sister's Circle.

"I'd really like you to come," she said.

But I didn't go. The next time I heard Cassie's voice it floated from a speaker as a large group gathered on the night of her death around the same fire circle where she had burned the coyote skin. Her voice punctuated the air as her signature song played: "Impermanence . . . That is all we really have. Impermanence . . . That is all we really have."

A glossy photo of a young woman with green eyes; a long mane of strawberry horse's hair, messily parted, tucked behind her left ear and hanging in front of her shoulders; a strong, square jaw; dimpled chin; thin lips drawn wide, exposing perfectly straight, white, square teeth. She sits on river stones, moonlight shimmering on the flowing water behind her: Terri

The night after Cassie died, I stood in Terri's kitchen, putting away clean dishes.

"What a shock," we said. "I can't believe she's gone."

I've often wondered if Terri and I were thinking the same thing: that for someone like Cassie—young, healthy, strong—to leave the planet before someone like Terri—tumor-laden and fading—defied the natural order.

Four photos of the same teenage boy:

> *He's dressed in a dark suit and cradles a plate of hors d'oeuvres in his left hand while giving a "thumbs up" with his right. His sandy brown hair is greased and combed over. A slight, closed-lipped smile curls up on one side of his mouth, the shadow of a mustache above his upper lip. The bottom right corner of the photo is punctured by border collie puppy chews.*
>
> *He stands erect in front of an evergreen tree, directly facing the camera, arms crossed over his chest, obstructing the view of the red and yellow dragon on his loose, black T-shirt. He wears baggy, faded jeans and tennis shoes. Wispy bangs cover his forehead. He smiles a direct, good-natured smile.*
>
> *He balances mid-action on the edge of a tilted skateboard in the middle of a bridge with no railings. His arms are stretched straight out from his folded body, slightly flexed at the elbows, fingers spread—like condor wings, as if with a few good flaps, he might lift off and fly away.*
>
> *He sits sideways on a rock in meadow grass, arms resting on his knees. His head is shaved, a shadow of new growth surfacing from a buzz cut. His dark brown eyes are reaching, reaching: Sean*

It wasn't because of Sean's good looks or resonant, baritone voice that he broke my daughter's heart. It was because he hanged himself in a tree outside his family's home. There is a myth that bones become stronger after they heal from a break, that in the process of healing, more bone grows in the place of the break than was there beforehand. What actually happens is calcium deposits at the site of the callus, mineralizing the point of fracture, which temporarily becomes stronger than the rest of the bone until it heals. Hearts aren't like bones. When a heart breaks, blood does not rush in to fill in the crack; it does not grow more flesh or become temporarily stronger. The place where Sean lives in my heart feels fractured, constricted, heavy as bone. Eight years later, the last thing it feels is stronger for the break.

I know it's morbid to call the box Death Box. Why not call it Memory Box or Keepsake Box? Isn't that how most people would regard a box full of relics? Death Box could be misconstrued to mean I intend the box for my ashes upon my death. Or the name could imply that it contains pieces of those who have already passed—which it does. I call it Death Box because besides holding random, miscellaneous things, it contains bits of others, bits of loved ones who have either passed from the world or transformed within the world, moved from one state of being to another.

> *A laminated business card-sized photo of a bald-shaven man in a maroon and gold robe, wearing oversized, boxy glasses: His Holiness the Dalai Lama, reincarnated manifestation of the Bodhisattva of Compassion, "teacher of an ocean of wisdom"*
> *A small box of "Animal Spirits Knowledge Cards": forty-eight thick, stiff cards representing animal totems, each with a painting by Susan Seddon Boulet, reproduced to "resonate with an ethereal energy and speak the language of the soul"*

I shuffle the cards, sifting a few on top, a few below, a few between. When the cards are held in a full deck, the edges align perfectly, creating a solid three-and-a-quarter-by-four-inch form, of which the edges no longer feel like that of forty-eight individual cards but a single unit—soft, smooth, glossy as burnished wood. With eyes closed, I turn over the top card. It reads:

Gull

Symbology: water, creation, emotions

"The gull, a creature of the sea and sky, symbolically links the lower, earthly world with the upper world of the spirit. It is also a symbol of unrestrained emotion . . . In the painting the gull appears along with a nautilus (mollusk) and the image of Amphitrite, the ancient Greek sea goddess who governs the emotions. The gull, nautilus, and goddess are all associated with water, the primordial element of creation and life."

I have this notion of carrying: carrying memories, carrying thoughts, carrying feelings. As if abstractions can take physical form, as if they can be made manifest to have weight, feel solid with mass, something to be carried. I have chopped wood and carried water, lived a life many consider "simple," despite the daily work necessary for survival. I still chop wood but no longer carry water. Instead, I carry objects forward through my life: this valentine, these strands of hair, these rings. But these objects need not constitute importance. To someone else they would mean nothing—an eyelash is just an eyelash, a handkerchief a piece of cloth, a photo, paper printed with ink.

I pack the bits and pieces back into the box. Leaving out the gull card, I prop it against the front. This will no longer be a Death Box; it will be an Ocean Box, governed by gull, protector of the shoreline, linking the earthly world with that of spirit, linking myself to the bits of others, to the memories I carry—like waves, rocking, pulsing, etching time.

SOMETHING TO DO WITH BALDNESS

Before you died, I never told you how I came to shave my head. We didn't have the opportunity. At that point, the how and the why of it seemed irrelevant. The only thing that mattered was that I was there with you, my friend. Your mother had just walked out the door. She huddled with a small group on the front porch, speaking in hushed, frantic whispers when I arrived, unrecognizable in my smooth, fuzzy baldness. Your partner thought I was a stranger until I got close. "Whoa," he said. "I didn't recognize you." I told him I had heard what happened—that your brother was discovered mysteriously dead in his apartment—and I was there to help. He handed me your baby. "Can you take her on a walk, please?" Her solid little body felt familiar in my arms, as if I were once again your caregiver, changing her diaper and feeding her a bottle of goat's milk because those chores had become too much for you. I strapped her into the stroller and headed down the gravel driveway. Your daughter delighted at going on a little jaunt and looking at the trees.

Your mother's visit was brief. She had arrived only the day before. But, of course, you know that. What you may not know is how torn up she was. Split down the middle. She probably put on a smile, patted your hand, and said she was sorry to leave, but she had to go bury your brother once the autopsy was concluded. Yet that couldn't have been how it went. What mother could smile and put on a good show for her dying daughter whom she'd only just seen for the first time in months? Or was it years? I don't recall her coming to see you earlier. But she must have met her little granddaughter before that. Maybe she slipped into the neighborhood when I wasn't paying attention. We had all been waiting for her to come, though none of us more than you.

Until I met her, I had strong feelings about your mother. I couldn't understand why she didn't come to take care of you, why she didn't even try to see you. Your best friend told me that your mother didn't handle stress well, that she avoided difficulties by numbing herself with alcohol. I never asked for confirmation of this gossip, but I have little reason to doubt its truth. When I stayed with you at Providence Medical Center while you were getting chemo—acting as nursemaid by emptying your bedpan and changing the pads beneath you, offering moral support by playing cards as the Grateful Dead serenaded us from the CD player—I told your mother you were sleeping when she called, although it was a morphine stupor really, and that she should call back. But what I wanted to say was that she was blowing it, that *she* should be here with you, not *me*, that *she* was the one you wanted. I wanted to tell her that during your fitful sleep the night before, you tossed your head from side to side, crying "Mommy, Mommy, Mommy" over and over and over again. All I could do was lie on the guest bed, unable to sleep, sorrow filling the cavity in my chest, helpless to soothe you because I was not the one. And in the morning, I didn't remind you of the night's occurrence. I figured your body and soul retained the knowledge of your desire. I didn't need to jog your memory.

Many people judged your mother. "She should have stayed," they said when she left for your brother's funeral. "She had a choice. She could have chosen the living over the dead." I, too, questioned her decision. Wouldn't it be better to spend time with the child who is still alive, but won't be for long, than go to the funeral of the one who is already gone? Such a decision I pray I will never have to face. But it's easy for those on the outside to pass judgment. Finally, she had come to see you, ten days before your death, when you no longer looked like the daughter she once knew. The tumor had disfigured your naked head, stretching the skin in a thin, splotchy, vein-lined mass, bubbled and glassy. And you were skinny. So skinny. Perhaps your resemblance to the Elephant Man made it easier for your mother to leave.

When I came back from strolling the baby, your mother was walking toward the car. She bent down to kiss her granddaughter and gazed at the baby's face, so like your own, set amidst a round, bald head. "It's hard to leave," she said.

I considered what she must be experiencing: losing two children almost simultaneously—one unexpectedly, the other not. "I'm so sorry," I said. "I can't imagine the pain you must be in. No one should have to go through this." Sometimes words fall short with a resounding hollow thud, like a coin dropped into a waterless wishing well.

"No, no one should have to go through this," your stepfather agreed. He held your mother by the elbow. I think she would have collapsed if his arm were not there.

"I don't know if I'm making the right decision," she said, her body swaying toward the aged, double-wide mobile home then toward the car. *Don't leave,* I wanted to say, but kept my silence. Your stepfather seemed to pull her along. I think he wanted to go. I guess sometimes facing death, packing it up neatly in a box and burying it, can be easier than facing life—or what's left of it.

I entered the house to find you sitting at your desk next to the kitchen, staring transfixed into space. Were you seeing your brother's spirit? Had he come to say he was waiting for you on the other side, not to fret because he would be there, that he had mysteriously died of natural causes and crossed over so you wouldn't be alone when your time came? You slowly turned your gaze toward me, without smiling, and patted your bald head. "Yes, I shaved it off," I said. You gave a slight nod. I moved about the kitchen, you giving nonverbal cues, pointing to what you wanted out of the refrigerator—a mango, lemon Recharge—me doing my best to interpret. I could see the gears shift in your mind as you struggled for words that would not come. You packed the bong, lit it, and inhaled the smoke, letting the marijuana soothe your pain, calm your anxiety, and stimulate your appetite. Somehow, in that moment, rather than feeling like I was caught in the midst of crisis, I simply felt like a woman hanging out with a friend, making the most of the time we had together.

I don't know what you thought about my bald head because we didn't talk about it. We didn't talk at all. But in that moment our silence held solidarity. We were the bald sisters, you and I, stripped down to the bare minimum, exposed, nothing left but pure essentials.

✺

Now, I will tell you how I came to shave my head.

A couple days before your brother died, I called Madrone and asked her to bring over her shaver. She was ecstatic and arrived immediately. It's not every day someone calls and asks to have her head shaved. She feared if she weren't quick, I'd change my mind. I sat on a bucket on the enclosed front porch with a towel around my neck and shoulders. She started at the nape of my neck, shaving underneath the top layers, which she left intact just in case I freaked and changed my mind. Then nobody would notice. We took a break so I could have time to adjust, and I walked onto the lawn and sat under the shade of the pine tree in the cool grass, leaned my head back and tossed my hair from side to side, feeling my long locks tickling my bare back. The breeze caressed my neck underneath the top layers of hair. It felt light and cool in the late spring warmth, and I was tempted to stop. The lighter load would help eliminate the sweat and stickiness of the summer heat. But in that moment, I knew that if I didn't proceed with shaving my head then I never would. I returned to the porch. "Shave the rest off," I said.

The blade buzzed in my ear like whirring mosquitoes. Hair slipped off in sections, falling to the redwood deck in swirls. Madrone changed the blade and skimmed my head to a sixteenth of an inch, not even enough fuzz to protect my skin from sunburn. My hand passed over the soft, smooth nap. Steve stared, bewildered and laughing. In the reflection of the window, I saw a woman who looked vaguely familiar.

It may sound odd, but shaving off my hair was an extemporaneous act. It included little contemplation and no conferring with my family. It included no ritual or calculated reasoning other than being the natural reflex to my turning thirty-five amidst your unwavering decline—a reality I could barely acknowledge and wished desperately I didn't have to. I did not say this to anyone. But in the back of my mind you were there, whispering your consent, where only I could hear.

I was scheduled for lunch duty at my girls' school that day. When I arrived, I greeted Lily, then twelve years old. "Hi, honey," I said.

She looked at me for a moment, puzzled, acquainted with the voice but not the head. She did a double take, then burst into tears. "What did you do?" she cried. "You look scary. Why did you do that?" Her anger escalated. "You don't look like my mom. I want my mom! How could you?"

I hadn't considered how my change of appearance would affect my children. Seven-year-old Akela stared. She did not express discontent the way her sister did. Akela's habit was to internalize her feelings and then express them bluntly. "You look stupid," she said. Eventually, the shock subsided, and Lily's sobs melted into laughter. The girls ran their hands over my scalp, feeling the soft bristle, marveling at their wacky mother. Still, they were pissed. "You should have told me you were going to do this," Lily said. "You look stupid," Akela repeated.

I suppose you didn't feel this, because for you, baldness wasn't a choice, but I felt a freedom in baldness. Gone was the need for shampoo and conditioner. Gone was the need for a brush and comb. I didn't have to tie my hair up when it got hot or worry about tangles from the wind. Rather, I experienced the wind dance around my face and never had to push strands out of my eyes. On the downside, it attracted attention. All kinds of attention. As you know from your own experience, baldness on a woman is a beacon the eyes are drawn to unwittingly.

Surprisingly, I had never been told I was beautiful as much as when I was bald. And the compliments all came from women. Heterosexual women. Imagine that! "Wow, you look so beautiful," I was told. "You have such a perfectly shaped head. It really brings out your eyes." Is that what it boils down to? Beauty is defined by the shape of one's head? Or is it that the symmetry of one's skull compliments or accentuates the symmetry of one's facial features? Not a single man registered this. Not even my husband. Oh, Steve agreed about the shape of my skull, but there were no undying proclamations of my beauty. Maybe men don't know what to do with a woman who rejects the social norms of femininity.

You were beautiful before you shaved your head. You were beautiful after. But beforehand you possessed long, thick wavy tresses of brilliant orange. Your hair hadn't always been wavy. It had been smooth and straight. It hadn't always been the color of pumpkin either. You went from strawberry-blond to carrot-top. For some reason chemo can change the color and texture of hair. Science hasn't determined exactly why. All I know is that chemotherapy is a poison cocktail that kills fast-growing cells, which includes hair follicles, and these drugs are designed to bring a person's body, your body, to the brink of death without actually killing. In a process like that, things are bound to go wonky.

During the six years of our friendship, I only ever knew you to be battling cancer, despite your moments of remission. The first time we spoke you were on crutches. You hadn't shaved your hair yet, just clipped it to above your shoulders in preparation for it to begin falling out. You had just begun the first of multiple chemotherapy sessions, and I brought you dinner. That was the way in our community. When someone gave birth, was ill, or suffered a loss, the thing to do was bring a meal. So I got on the list. But, I had an ulterior motive. I wanted to meet you because we shared a mutual best friend.

At first I was wary of you, slightly threatened. You had stolen my friend's heart, and it was obvious that the two of you were closer than she and I ever would be. Some bonds can't be fabricated. You two had *it*, that special we-can-tell-each-other-anything-we're-there-for-each-other-no-matter-what-nothing-can-break-us-apart bond. I was nervous to connect but figured if she loved you so much, you must have something special. Lucky for me, I didn't procrastinate. For if I had, it would have been like looking in the wrong direction as a brilliant shooting star streaked across the sky, only to turn my head in time to see the tail fizzle.

I had seen you a few times before we met—once at the Oregon Country Fair, once at the Grange, once at Lily's school. You had taken a job as an aide in her kindergarten. Lily bonded with you instantly, following you around, sitting by you, holding your hand. And you responded with mutual adoration. You spent only one week in the classroom. It was Halloween. There was a pumpkin walk through the fall garden, vegetation turned brown and yellow, grasses dried up, flower stalks standing exhausted and still. The ground was damp from the previous night's rain, the air moist and fleshy. Jack-o-lanterns—some scary, some cute—lined the pathways. The kids were singing. You were dressed all in black—a velvet broomstick skirt that hung to your ankles, a long sleeve shirt, and a conical witch's hat that pointed toward the sky. Your long, red-tinged hair hung from beneath the stiff brim of the hat, framing your narrow face and resting on your shoulders. You held a Native American drum in one hand and beat it with your other in time to the children's voices. *Earth my body, water my blood, air my breath, and fire my spirit.* Lily stood by your side. A few days later I heard you were not going to be working in the classroom. You had been to a doctor and discovered the lump on your leg to be a tumor.

I wasn't prepared for the reaction to my baldness at the Grower's Market. It was early morning—around 6:30—when I arrived to set up my weekly booth space to sell plants from our nursery, so I wore a hat to keep warm. As the temperature rose, I took off my hat. No one said anything—aloud; however, their eyes reflected fear, so I felt I should explain. "I'm turning thirty-five and I got a bee up my butt and decided to shave my head," I said.

Relief washed over their faces, relaxing their tightened muscles.

"Oh, thank goodness."

"I thought you must be going through chemotherapy," said one person.

"Yeah," said another. "I was really worried."

And then, "But why else would you shave your head?"

Cancer.

This might shock you, but I hadn't imagined people would think I had cancer, although it's a common assumption about a bald woman. Those who knew me well were curious. "What made you do it?" they asked. When that question came from our mutual friends, I was confused. Wasn't it obvious? Becoming bald was an act of solidarity with you. That was certainly an important part of the equation. But there was more to it than that. I was turning thirty-five. We were the same age. You were dying. I was not. Shaving my head was a response to facing mortality. I wasn't fully aware of this at the time. Clear, accurate words failed me, so I would say, "I'm having a midlife crisis." Yes, that was it, I convinced myself—even though thirty-five is a bit young for a midlife crisis. Why else would I shave my head, driven by an angst I had not felt since I was a hormonal teen and a deep-seated need to reclaim my youth? A few days after shaving my head, on my birthday, I had my nose pierced, an age-old ritual that now serves as a contemporary means of feeling pain—and thus feeling alive.

I already knew what you planned to tell me as we walked that day, about a year and a half before your death, on the dirt road winding through evergreens above my house. In small communities, gossip travels like black crows meandering from farm to farm, seeking scraps and casting a shadowy pall on daily life. The news you shared signaled the end of your remission.

"There's a tumor in my leg," you said.

Again, I thought.

"It's small."

So far.

"I'm going to see a healer in the Southwest. She does hands-on healing and coughs up tumors out of people's bodies."

We ambled through the forest, deep green with privacy, peace and quiet whispering promises of . . . what? Promises that everything would be okay? That the tumor would disappear and not return? That this healer would somehow magically sever the tumor cells knitted to your bone and cough up the tumor like a cat does a hairball? I nodded encouragingly, asked questions, remained supportive. Who was I to say this couldn't be it, the one thing that might actually work? I hoped and prayed this healer was the real deal. "Wow, that's great," I said. "When do you leave?" Internally, I questioned whether your pregnancy was responsible for growth beyond that of a baby.

You weren't supposed to get pregnant. The doctor may not have actually said this, but some of us thought it. We didn't dare say so—it was your decision, your life. Still, we believed that pregnancy would aggravate the cancer. It made sense to us. In the cycle of human growth, cells grow, divide, and make new cells continuously. Normally, our bodies are able to control the process as new cells are created to replace old and damaged cells. But when cells grow and divide out of control, they become abnormal, group together, and form a tumor. All those hormones coursing through your body, stimulating growth of a fetus, stimulated those cancer cells. I've always wondered if you suspected this too. One bright summer day, Steve and I came to your house and found you working in the garden, one of your favorite things to do, and you waddled over with your seven-month-pregnant belly. "I have something to tell you guys," you said. "There's a tumor in my head, and I have to go to Seattle to have it removed."

You really wanted to have a baby. No matter the cost. I understand your desire to experience pregnancy and childbirth, to grow round with a rolling, kicking life force. I can even understand why you would choose it, knowing the possibility that it could shorten your time here. Well, I can *try* to understand. I imagine having a baby was the best way to ensure you wouldn't disappear. Creating life, passing on your genes, must have seemed the perfect way to prove you existed, to leave your mark. And what an indelible mark you left. You sacrificed yourself to give life to your daughter, to continue the cycle. But was it a selfless sacrifice? She has no memory of you. For many years, she will remain motherless. Until a time, years from now, a new woman will come to town and step into the role, for no other reason than a bond will form between them. And then some years later, your daughter will give birth to a daughter of her own.

What is motherhood? Is it the offering of one's body in the production of a child, or is it the day-to-day grind of raising an infant to childhood to adolescence to adulthood? Or is it both? And what of the mothers who live but do not make themselves available to their young, no matter their child's age? You were thirty-five and dying—without the presence of your mother. In essence, you, too, were motherless.

Her picture sat in a frame on the rolling table next to your hospital bed, a miniature, bald you. When the nurse came to take your vitals and check the monitors, she asked, "Is that your baby?" You proudly responded, "Yes, isn't she cute?"

"Yes, she is. She looks like you," the nurse said. And then a sad, uncomfortable expression overcame her face.

On the oncology ward, nurses administer chemotherapy treatments all the time that have absolutely no curative effects. The doctors had no viable remedy for your rare sarcoma, so rather than offer you no options, they suggested chemo. Your nausea was excruciating, and the chemo drugs combined with the morphine to manage your pain made you trip worse than any psychedelic ever could. "I don't want to do it," you said to me. "I don't want to go there. It's a really bad trip. I'm afraid I'll never come back."

What could I say to that? I didn't want you to go there either.

"Please don't give me any more," you cried when the nurse came to administer the next dose. "Please . . . "

"You want to get better, don't you?" the nurse said. "You need the chemo to get rid of the cancer. So you can go home to your baby."

These were empty words made by a nurse performing her duties. She had to say it—to get you to take the drugs. But the chemo was futile to affect the football-sized tumor in your femur. And I suspect you and the nurse thought so too. Yes, you would go home to your baby. But for how long?

Sometimes family doesn't come in the form of blood relations. You had been fighting tumors for six years. Part of your bone had been removed from your leg and a metal rod inserted to connect the lower and upper parts of your tibia. You had gone through chemotherapy twice. The rare sarcoma had spread from your tibia to your femur to your head. And we—your friends—saw you through it all. We drove you to doctor's appointments, stayed with you in the hospital, had you transported to the emergency room when an infection rather than the cancer threatened to be your demise. We washed your dishes, cleaned your house, did your laundry. We cared for your baby girl when you were too tired and weak. Through all that time, through all those many months of pain and suffering and choices, it wasn't your family who attended you. It was us, your friends. So when your blood relatives did show up, we knew it must be close to the end.

You were working on a scrapbook for your little one and had someone call to see if I had beading needles you could borrow. I rushed over,
knowing that I better take advantage of any opportunity to see you. You
were sitting in your rocking chair in the living room. I knelt on the floor
at your feet as you showed me the scrapbook cover you had embroi-
dered. We talked awhile. I don't know what about, but you were lucid,
more so than when I had seen you the week before, the day your mother
left. It was afternoon, and the hot June sun reflected off the pond like
shards of broken glass. And then it happened. All of a sudden. The mass
in your head got too heavy. Your spindly neck couldn't sustain the weight
and teetered your head off balance. You began to fall backward and to
the side, over the arm of the rocking chair. You could not stop gravity.
Your eyes widened in fear. You started to moan. It took only a second,
but I watched it happen in slow motion, you leaning, falling, about to go
down. My hands reached out and grabbed you, supporting your head
from behind, stabilizing your neck. I yelled for your partner, and he came
running. You were exhausted, we agreed. You needed to lie down and
rest, take a nap.

We supported you as you stood on your good leg and swiveled into the
wheelchair, ready to be pushed down the narrow hallway. As we left the
brightness of the living room and approached the darkened bedroom at the
end of the hall, the light faded the way it does when you enter a tunnel. We
situated the wheelchair next to the bed and helped you under the covers,
tucking them in around your shrunken frame. I told you to have a good
sleep; I'd see you next time.

Next time never came. With your partner, I had tucked you into bed for
the last time.

Several days later I got the call that you had gone, and I went to gather
with the others at your house. When I entered that darkened bedroom,
there you were, lying on top of the covers, a grey, sunken skeleton. I could
not believe that in only a few days you had deteriorated that much more.
Your body had been bathed, dressed in fresh clothing—your favorite purple
dress—and you were decorated with flowers: calendula petals scattered all
over the bed, rosebuds meticulously placed along your arms, down your
legs, over your heart. We were clumsy, those of us who remained with
you. The finality pressed in on us like the walls of a shrinking room. Your
best friend held her camera, taking shot after shot, immortalizing you like
a deity on a shrine. And I wondered what she would ever do with these

photographs. Who would want to look at them? But that camera in her hands gave her something to hold on to, kept her from dissolving.

Later, on market day, a couple of women came by the booth, looking at the vegetable starts and flowers. One of the women wore a scarf covering her bare head. "Aren't you afraid you're going to get sunburned?" she asked, looking at my bald head.

"No," I said. "I just put on sunscreen."

"Don't you feel self-conscious?"

"Not really. I like it. It feels good."

"Are you all through with your chemo?" she asked.

"Oh . . . I'm not going through that," I said.

"You're not?" She looked at me, uncomprehending.

I shook my head. Awkwardness grabbed me and turned me inside out. Here I stood, a woman essentially bald for no obvious reason. And there she stood, a woman on whom baldness had been forced. *Why?* she wanted to know.

How do I tell someone who is battling cancer that my baldness is self-imposed? The pat answer—midlife crisis—seemed a petty and trivialized half-truth. And to mention that I had done it in solidarity with my dying friend seemed cruel. For what cancer-afflicted person wants to be reminded her condition could be fatal? So I didn't mention you. I didn't say that I had a very good friend born as I was in the year of the horse, a fellow '66 baby, who had left the planet and that shaving my head seemed a natural way to show my love and support. I didn't say that shaving my hair off was symbolic of the letting go I now dealt with, a facing of the harsh fact that I had the opportunity to watch my children grow, to know them and let them know me, while you did not. I didn't say that I struggled with the realization that it could have been me but wasn't, and that the mysteriousness of life made me angry and distressed and confused. Instead I said, "I always wanted to shave my head, but it was never the right time. It feels really free and easy. All I have to do is wash and wear. And a lot of people tell me it's beautiful."

"I wish I had your guts," she said and wandered off to look at other booths.

Toward the end of the market, she came back, scarf off, head held high, smiling. Her slumped shoulders replaced by a confident, more relaxed stance.

"Hey, you took your scarf off," I said.

"Yeah." She rubbed her hand over her bare skin. "You inspired me."

My hair is long now, though not as long as before I shaved it. I've started going to a stylist, not often, only twice a year, for a cut and color. Eventually the gray starts to seep through again, like silver threads in a weaving's weft. At first I kind of like it, the sprinkling. It makes me look mature, I think, in that Carol King "Natural Woman" sort of way—strong, experienced, wise. But after too long, the gray begins to take over, in that coarse, frizzy, crazy lady sort of way. That's when I make the appointment. The stylist always comments on the cover up. "I'd recommend a demi-permanent color," she'll say. No matter if it's the same hairdresser or someone new, she always focuses on the gray. "It will take care of those unruly hairs that want to stick out all over the place," she'll say. It's her job to reinforce insecurity in one's aging. If she didn't, she'd have fewer clients. But why the shame in looking older? Why not celebrate the fact that I have lived long enough to see my hair change color? I wonder, if you were still here, would your hair be changing too? Or would you still look like a Celtic goddess? I hear redheads don't turn gray unless they shave their hair off.

I saw them recently, your partner and daughter. It was a fluke really. Motivated by nostalgia, I went to the children's toy store at the mall even though I have no more young ones to shop for. And there they were.

She was grown up, preadolescent, hair the color of yours before the chemo—golden straw with a twang of berry—and the same face, your face. She didn't recognize me. She had no idea who I was. She ran right past me between the stickers and the rubber dinosaurs, and I watched her search the aisles, hands fingering the merchandise, eyes intent. She came to where I stood talking with her father, turning on her best daddy's-girl charm: "Can I get something? A puzzle or a game?"

I can hear you ask me that question, the one you asked more than once, first in the hospital and then months later at home: "Will she be okay? Will he take good care of her?"

There is something I have to tell you. At your memorial, I lied. Not intentionally. Nevertheless, it became a lie. When my turn came to speak, I said I would be there for your baby; I would be her auntie, help raise her. In that moment, I truly believed myself.

But I didn't. I haven't. I couldn't.

Reprieve: Winter

First thing in the morning, I step outside to take a shower and find it frozen. This happens when we forget to leave the faucet running at night. Typically, it is the narrow, vertical pipe that stands upright from the bathtub faucet to the showerhead that freezes. Sometimes, if I'm not in a hurry to bathe, I'll just go back inside and wait for the temperature to rise and the pipe to thaw. This is not always practical. Some days are too cold and it never thaws at all, or it takes too long and I don't have the time to wait. That's when I put the kettle on the stove to boil. I pour the boiling water over the faucet valves first so I can turn the hot valve on fully; then I pour the water up and down the pipe and over the shower head. I hear slight cracking sounds as the ice inside the pipe begins to loosen and separate itself from the metal. Eventually the water begins to flow, first only a few drizzles and then a full spray.

We don't have a bathroom. We have the outdoor tub and shower, and we have what I call an "indoor outhouse," a composting outhouse consisting of two side-by-side, five-foot-deep chambers above ground, built from cinder blocks on a concrete floor. It has insulated walls, a small window for air, and a roof and is accessible through a multipurpose room built to be a bathroom but never finished due to lack of funds.

Often, in the morning, there is a layer of ice coating the bottom of the tub. When it snows, the tub fills and instead of shoveling it out, I run the shower and the hot water dissolves the snow, which disappears down the drain. A few times, I have been greeted by dead bats and live mice. Once, we put one of the cats in the tub to catch the mouse, who then ran in erratic circles. The cat was more concerned with being in a bathtub than chasing the mouse, but the mouse did not know this and dove down the drain.

We dismantled the pipe from the outside, and the soggy, defeated-looking mouse climbed out carefully and crept under the house.

Sometimes, bathing commences in the rain. There is nothing to be done for it except strip off my clothes and let water wash me clean from all directions. The hot spray intermingles with a cool mist, a gentle sprinkle, plump drops, or pelting hard pricks that feel like an attack from minute shards of ice. I have even been caught in a hailstorm.

The first moments are the hardest. The peeling of layers to expose skin to frigid temperatures. The sharp inhalation of breath. The chilled feet on hard, frosted ground. I'd like to believe that bathing in the cold makes for a hardy constitution and an indomitable spirit. It certainly is not for the faint of heart. Nowadays, the few times I take a bath elsewhere, I feel a bit claustrophobic, hemmed in by walls, no view, and a lack of fresh air. If given the opportunity, I don't know that I'd trade my outdoor bathing for the conventional. I think I much prefer open sky where at night, bats slip from the house's cracks and flap overhead in irregular patterns and an occasional shooting star glides through the galaxy, where the moon and Milky Way slowly shift their locations in comparison to the silhouettes of trees.

The tub once stood sentry in a field, a watering trough for cattle or horses, maybe sheep or goats—a footless claw-foot bathtub. A cast iron statue of sorts, it has a lusterless white porcelain interior chipped on the bottom in two places that look like tree rings. It is both deep and long and reclines at one end, with a rolled rim perfectly molded for the grip of a human hand. The rusty gray exterior desperately needs a paint job, or better yet, a sheath of knotty pine paneling. How long had it sat quenching the parched tongues of gritty, toothed muzzles? Did it languish in dusty, flaky earth; on hard, weedy ground; or in the mud? Maybe it was a social meeting place, like an office watercooler, where animals exchanged pleasantries about the way the sun glistened or how the breeze cooled their backs against the stiff air.

Steve bought the tub for twenty-five dollars from Morrow's, a recycled building supply shop run by a guy who dismantled time-worn barns, cabins, and farmhouses in exchange for oak flooring, cedar paneling, French doors, and wooden-framed, stained-glass windows. Morrow salvaged porcelain sinks, stainless steel faucets, brass hinges, and glass doorknobs, even fireplace mantles, chandeliers, and, yes, bathtubs. He sold the tub cheap because it wasn't worth the work of restoring, and well, what good is a claw-foot tub with no feet?

When we first got it, the tub lived in our one-room cabin set on bricks and boards. Shortly after Akela was born, in an effort to create more space, the tub went outside. At one point, we didn't have to worry about pipes freezing because the tub faucet had rusted through where it connects to the cold handle, and a stream of water steadily leaked. Now, a swivel valve turns the cold on and off. And even though the hose feeding the cold water and the pipe from the on-demand propane water heater are both wrapped in condensed polyethylene insulation, we let the faucet drip on the coldest days and nights of winter in defense against freezing and cracking pipes.

Steve is a bath man. He clears the tub of any debris the wind has brought and turns the valve to make the stream of water as hot as can be. Because the cast iron absorbs and holds the cold, no matter how hot the water filling the tub is, it cools considerably until the tub has equalized, transforming the cold iron by absorbing the heat of the water. Steve helps the process along by pouring kettles of boiled water into the tub until he's satisfied with the temperature. For him, bath time is meditation time. He listens to kirtan and sings with the long chants until the water cools. I like to go out to the porch and peek around the doorframe at him. This is when he looks the most peaceful. His face flushes crimson beneath his beard and mustache, and a softness settles on his forehead, the creases eased, his receding hairline exposed from his long, wet hair smoothed back. Seeing me, he grins, and the blue of his eyes sparkles in the crisp, winter, evening air.

I HAVE TO TELL YOU

Though it be honest, it is never good
To bring bad news: give to a gracious message
An host of tongues, but let ill tidings tell
Themselves when they be felt.

—William Shakespeare

I.

Ten years old:

Standing behind the Green Gables Elementary School library with my best friend, Marnie.

"There is something I have to tell you."

The small patch of grass, shorn, electric green from too much fertilizer, the blades sneaking up around and between my toes as my feet squish into the soil beneath, sopping wet from a timed sprinkler system set for too long. Heat radiates off the cement wall of the library, the cerulean sky in this Bay Area town always a bit too sunny. I've never done this before. I'm not sure how to begin. Marnie saying, "What? What happened?" in her high-pitched voice, words fast and pressing.

Marnie missed gymnastics the day the team was told. All of us girls sat on the scratchy, carpeted gym floor. Gina, one of our three coaches, leaned against the wall, ramrod straight but shuddering, her eyes red and scrunched and barely visible through tears, staccato sound vibrations puffing out through her lips: huhuhuhuhuh. Bruce, the head coach, said the words straight out, deadpan: Cathy (our third coach) would be gone for a while. He didn't know when she'd come back, if ever. She went to Hawaii. Over the weekend, her fiancé, Neil, had died in a car accident.

Neil. Sweet, tall, goofy Neil, with his fine, brown hair parted down the middle that hung in straight wisps to his chin, framing his narrow face and long nose and gap-toothed grin. Neil, our play buddy, who wore jeans and cowboy boots and tight, worn T-shirts or button-up plaid with the sleeves rolled up. A posse of keys clipped to one of his belt loops jangled at his hip. Our game: steal the keys—a real feat, for Neil was quick on the draw. Marnie and I would circle him, hyenas moving in for the kill, laughing, always laughing, each of us lunging in turns, grabbing for the clip as Neil twirled on the spot, reaching an arm out to tickle us, him smiling, always smiling.

Except one time I tried to play with him he did not smile.

Our gym team had been invited to be the halftime entertainment at a 49ers game at Candlestick Park. During the game, we hung out at the end zone, and every time the 49ers scored or made a good play, we jumped on the mini-tramp and did flips onto a mat. At halftime, we tumbled on the artificial turf and jumped up and down waving our arms, yelling, "Go 49ers! Go 49ers!"

On the way home, I sat on the front bench seat next to the passenger door, with Neil driving and my coach, Cathy, in the middle. Three other girls were sitting in the back seat of the four-door sedan. We were heading south on Highway 101, the smell of fishy bay marsh and saltwater breeze whirling in through the half open windows. Maybe it was my intoxication from the air, maybe it was my giddiness from the game, maybe it was just that when it came to Neil, I morphed into a rambunctious gremlin. But for some unknowable reason, other than I thought it would be funny, I reached across Cathy's lap, grabbed the steering wheel, and yanked it down up, down up, down up. In a flash, Neil's hand slapped my forearm. I let go as his clear blue eyes glared and he growled, "Don't ever do that again." All my high energy devilishness seeped away. I retreated against the door and stared out the window, ashamed to look at Neil.

A few months later, behind the school library: "There is something I have to tell you."

Marnie anxiously waiting. "What? What happened?"

"Neil is dead. He died in a car crash." Guilt rolls over me like an ocean wave.

There is something I don't want to tell you. As a young girl, every time I think of Neil's death, I feel my hand on the steering wheel. My young girl's brain stitches these two events together into one cloth: Neil dying in a car accident, me yanking on the wheel.

II.

Thirty-four years old:

Busy getting my children ready for school. The phone rings. It's my friend Betsy. She says, "Did you hear what happened?"

"No, what is it?"

"Cassie is dead. She died in a car accident."

I'm confused. It sounds like she said Kathy. "Who?"

"Cassie."

Why would she be calling to tell me about Cassie? I wonder. She is not close friends with her. But she is close with Kathy. That must be who she is talking about. "Kathy?"

"Cassie."

"I'm sorry I can't understand you. Are you saying Kathy or Cassie?"

"Cassie."

This is important. I want to be sure I get this right, but I still can't tell which name she is saying. "Can you please spell it?" Betsy releases an exasperated sigh.

"C-A-S-S-I-E, with an S, as in Sam."

Steve watches me struggle through this exchange. After I learn the basic details—Cassie died in a car accident on Highway 89 on her way to Reno to visit family—I hang up the phone and prepare to tell Steve. Despite the fact that he overheard my side of the conversation and can guess what I am going to say, I feel apprehensive. Steve really liked Cassie. I mean *really* liked her. She was short and cute and sweet, with a sparkle in her large hazel eyes, and every time she was around, he would get this shy, crushed-out expression, and he'd say, "Hi Cassie," in that school-boy tone at one time reserved only for me.

There is something I don't want to tell you. For the briefest moment after hearing the news, as I say the words to Steve, a troublesome thought flits across my consciousness: *at least now I won't have to worry about my husband's attraction.*

III.

Thirty-six years old:

Just arisen from my tent where I'm camped at a women's gathering, stumbling bleary-eyed to the outdoor breakfast line early Sunday morning. Two friends intercept me before I cross the bridge over the creek. "Hey Laurie," they say, "Come here."

What is it? I wonder.

We sit down on a faded, dirty, white and purple throw rug that flattens the patchy grass into the dirt near the fire pit: smooth, dark river rocks entombing powdery, gray ashes and chunks of charred wood. They tell me my friend Marlin's husband had a heart attack and died. After hearing this, I lose my appetite, but I continue to the breakfast line anyway.

Lynne, a six-foot-three Amazon to my four-foot-eleven pixie, towers over me. She has just gotten her plate filled.

"There is something I have to tell you." I move with her, far from the circles of women sitting in sheared meadow grass. She sways on long legs, plate of food in hand.

"Let's sit down," I say. Closer to eye level, she looks at me expectantly. I can't put it off any longer; I have to tell her. "Vine died of a heart attack yesterday." Vine, despite being our friend Marlin's husband, is the father of one of Lynne's daughter's best friends. "There was no warning," I say. "He just dropped dead."

Dropped dead. That is a crass way to put it. But there is a reason for such phrases: accuracy. It sounds flippant, but that's the way it was. Or so I hear. Without being aware of it, Vine had something seriously wrong with his heart. Earlier in the day, he had visited one of his daughters, and when she hugged him goodbye, she heard an irregularity in its beats. Stress had been building for some time, and for whatever reason, the exertion of standing from where he sat in his best friend's living room pinnacled into his sudden collapse from cardiac arrest.

"I'm sorry to be the one to tell you," I say to Lynne, because that's what people say—no one wants to be the bearer of bad news. Don't shoot the messenger.

I think about how the night before we had all been gathered in the lodge for the talent show, and midstream a procession of women ushered Marlin out of the building. I thought it a curious action at the time. Marlin's closest friends gathered around her, the way I imagine a pod of dolphins escorts a troubled swimmer out of shark-infested waters. *Something is up,*

I had thought. I did not imagine it could be something so drastic, so unexpected. The most likely possibility seemed it had something to do with Marlin's breast cancer, for she was due to begin chemotherapy the following Monday.

Later that afternoon, when the women's gathering has ended, I give Lynne a ride home. We stop at Marlin's house first, so Lynne can check on her daughter, who is there supporting her friend. I park the truck, and we trudge up the hill to the house. From outside, we can hear a small commotion within. Lynne goes in while I stand there quietly, not wanting to intrude. Marlin and Vine's eldest, grown daughter comes out the front door.

"Hi Laurie, come in, come in," she whispers urgently, waving her arm around me, ushering me inside. I did not plan on this. I only brought Lynne to check on her daughter. Like the messenger, I am just the ride. Still, I let myself be scooped in because resisting would be more awkward. I sit right inside the door, against the wall, hugging my knees, trying to blend into the carpet.

The living room is muted, with lights on only in the adjoining open-air kitchen. Marlin and Vine's youngest, teenage daughter lies on the floor, encircled by women. Marlin kneels at her daughter's feet, face white, shocked. "Why did he leave me? Why did he leave me?" her daughter moans.

He did not only leave her. He left a wife, three daughters, a grandson. But this daughter is so despondent, in this moment her grief overshadows anyone else's pain. The encircling women have their hands on the girl, stroking, soothing. "Shhhhhh," they say. Someone places a damp cloth on the girl's forehead. She lies there delirious, a moaning limp body of grief.

Lynne's daughter sits at her friend's head. She glances up at her mother, tears streaming down a contorted pink face that says *help me, Mama; I don't know how to do this.* And I do not wish to see this. I do not wish to be privy to the acute pain of this daughter's loss, her mother and friends at her side. I am an intruder to heartache, an unwilling witness to loss. I am just the driver.

"Why did he leave me? Why did he leave me?" her voice strangles, pleads. She wants an answer. There is no answer. Her sister, the one who ushered me in, busies herself in the kitchen. Food = comfort. Action keeps the body busy, numbing the mind and heart.

There is something I don't want to tell you. I can't stand it, witnessing this pain, feeling it penetrate my skin. I feel as though I am underwater, and the pressure of the depths is pushing in on me, threatening to burst my lungs. So I escape. I go back outside to wait where I can breathe.

IV.
Forty years old:

I'm the mother of a twelve-year-old daughter who is hospitalized after emergency abdominal surgery, sitting vigil at my daughter's bedside. She is recovering not only from surgery but a raging infection that circulates through her bloodstream. Ruptured appendix + two quarts pus = sepsis, an inflammatory response that threatened to shut down her organs. Before she was moved here, to this room on the ninth floor of Doernbecher Children's Hospital, the intensive care unit doctor on call told an optimistic me, "She is not out of the woods yet," squelching my hope in an attempt to impress upon me the severity of the situation. "She is not out of the woods yet" = "your daughter is still in critical condition; she might not make it." But sitting by her unconscious side—listening to the constant beeps of monitors; watching the monotonous moving green, white, and blue lines indicating her heart rate, respirations, and percent of oxygen concentration; an oxygen cannula and tube in her nose, suctioning green bile from her belly; intravenous plastic tubing in her hands; a catheter bag full of pee the color of dark amber beer—the only way I survived the PICU was to believe that every second the antibiotics dripped through her IV, her condition improved.

Though the immediate danger passed and she is no longer in the PICU, she remains on a triple cocktail of intravenous antibiotics. As I watch from the built-in bed/window seat, my friend Yarrow calls.

"I hear Akela almost died," she says.

"Yes," I tell her, "it was a very close call."

Then without warning, without saying, there is something I have to tell you, Yarrow says: "Did you know that Hanneli passed away yesterday?"

Hanneli: striking, blonde, German beauty with a smile that stretched across the valley; yoga master; and friend—and five-year sufferer of a brain tumor. I picture Hanneli's mother, how she came with her daughter to our plant nursery on Mother's Day years earlier to buy flowers and vegetable starts, and I think, *now she will never again spend Mother's Day with her only daughter.* This reality came too close to being my own. All I want is to push it away, sever myself from the possibility. In this moment, I feel angry at Yarrow for divulging such news to me here, now.

There is something I don't want to tell you. This is what I say to Yarrow: "No, I didn't know that." But this is what I think: *Thank god it wasn't* my *daughter.*

SOJOURNS WITH BIG CATS IN TRIPTYCH

I.

The rental property where we lived when Lily was born was not that re-mote, but access was a challenge. The first half of the road, while straight and flat, was full of deep, rutted potholes. During the last trimester of my pregnancy, rather than be jostled in the car, I got out and walked the quar-ter mile before crossing the wood-plank-and-cable suspension bridge hov-ering over the creek.

Walking across the bridge was not bad but driving across took getting used to. The gravel road sloped upward before dropping down onto the curved bridge, so you couldn't see where you were headed, kind of like driving off a cliff. You had to have faith the tires would land on the two planks and not in the grooves on either side. Then there was the bouncing and swaying once the vehicle landed on the old wood boards. Exiting was much the same, sloping upward over a threshold before dropping down again. There was relief, though, because no matter where you landed upon exiting, it would be on solid ground.

The driveway climbed a hillside so steep that at one critical juncture, a slab of pavement had been placed to initiate tire traction and prevent cars from sliding backward down the hillside. All these factors made the prop-erty, bordered by public lands, a solitary space for wildlife.

One afternoon, while caring for my infant daughter, a neighbor from around the mountain arrived at our back steps on horseback. "Do you have a phone?" she asked. "There's a cougar in the woods back here that is very ill. I think we should call Fish and Game."

She told us how she and her son were traversing the mountainside on their horses when they saw movement in the bushes. A cougar was lying in the dry leaves of the oaks and madrones, convulsing. She showed Steve where the animal lay, only a few hundred feet behind our house. When he returned, he said, "That cougar isn't going to live long."

I had never seen a cougar in the wild, and the prospect intrigued me. "I want to see it," I said, so he described how to find it. I left Lily in his care and went searching in the woods.

When I arrived, the cougar was dead.

It lay camouflaged in the dry, crackling leaves, its eyes wide open but sunken into its skull and rolled backward slightly. Its mouth remained a snarl of bared fangs. The sandy-colored coat had no luster. Its body was emaciated. I slowly inched closer, hesitant, even though I knew there was no life left. This powerful hunter had once been full of grace and ferociousness. The threat was now gone, yet I still felt vulnerable in such close proximity. I felt disappointed to see its lifeless body still and without breath, and relieved those piercing eyes, frozen in a painful fury, could no longer see me.

II.

I awoke to horrific screaming. It wasn't human screaming, although it sounded like a woman being raped and tortured or possibly a baby being torn to shreds. It was blood-curdling, sending shivers up the spine. My body tensed. I wrapped the quilt tighter around myself, held my breath, lay still, listened. More painful shrieking, as I imagined limbs being ripped, shredded. Since becoming a mother, I had also become a light sleeper, my subconscious trained to listen for subtle sounds: a choke, a muffled cry, a murmur from a bad dream. Murderous shredding didn't top the list of usual nighttime sounds, and I nudged Steve and whispered, "Steve, are you awake?" He grumbled. How he managed to sleep through such a sound baffled me, especially as we were living in an uninsulated school bus while we built a cabin on our newly purchased property. "Steve, do you hear that?"

"What?"

A high-pitched screech pierced from the uphill side of the meadow, an arrow shooting night terrors through the forest, hitting its bull's eye in one of the nearby trees. "That," I said.

He sat up in bed and said, "What is it?"

"I don't know. But it sounds terrible. Go check it out." Toddler Lily slept undisturbed on one side of the futon, which was wedged in the back of the bus on wooden pallets on the floor, flush against the back-door emergency exit.

Steve grabbed the flashlight and stumbled down the aisle, past rough-hewn kitchen shelves, an aluminum sink set in two by four framing, and a worn blue lounge chair next to an upturned wooden utility-cable spool used for a table. He reached the driver's seat just past the rusty woodstove and pulled the lever that opened the folding passenger door. He hadn't turned on the flashlight yet. The night was jet black; there were no shadows. I heard him descend the two steps at the bus's opening and move forward a few paces on the withered grass before turning on the flashlight. The button clicked, and a beam of light cut through the air. "Oh shit!" Steve cried. He bounded back up the steps, shut the door with a frantic swing of the lever, and ran to the back of the bus.

"What happened?"

"Something ran straight at me when I turned on the light. It went up that tree." Steve gestured with the flashlight to the tree standing next to the bus. "I also heard a large animal go up the knoll. I think it was a cougar."

"What ran into the tree?"

"I'm not sure." Steve peered out the window and shined the light up into the tree. There, in the crook of a branch, a few feet from the back of the bus, sat a masked bandit. "It's a raccoon. And it looks like its tail is missing."

The next morning the tailless raccoon sat curled on the branch, dark face weary, body bedraggled. The poor thing merely glanced at us like an indifferent housecat perched on a window ledge in sunshine, without the crisp flick of a tail. It showed no fear. It seemed comforted by our active presence. We were the light at the end of its tunnel, what saved the hunted from the hunter. The tree the raccoon rested in was directly above the chicken coop. I decided it posed no risk, so I let the chickens loose for the day. As the clucking birds pranced out of the cage and scratched for bugs in the dirt, the raccoon turned its head to follow their path, the most deliberate movement it made the entire day.

III.

The forest is a black vacuum of silence at new moon, and no lingering haze of light from town exists because town is twenty-five miles away.

I sat up in the darkness. Cougar screaming had chilled me awake. And even though this time I knew its source, the sound was as daunting and creepy as the last time I heard it those many years before. I checked to see if my cat, Lacey, was lying on the bed in her usual spot but felt nothing. I feared she was outside about to become cougar-snack, so I slipped out of bed. I went out the back door, navigating my way, via flashlight, to our gravel driveway.

The rocks were rough on my bare feet, and jagged edges dug into my soles. Scanning the flashlight back and forth along the driveway, I moved slowly over the shale. The night's coolness settled on my pale skin. "Here, kitty, kitty," I called, clicking my tongue—tut, tut, tut—in my usual way. My mind was singular: find Lacey. Tut, tut, tut, I clicked. "Here, kitty, kitty," my soprano voice sang. I walked the three hundred feet to the curve in the road still calling, "Here kitty, kitty," still swinging my flashlight from right to left then right again. Then I stopped, suddenly consumed by anxiety. I felt nocturnal eyes scrutinizing me from behind. I thought, *There is a big cat nearby. It can see me, but I can't see it.* All I wanted to do was get back to the house. I wanted to run, but I knew running was wrong. All the warnings say to make yourself look as large as possible, pull a sweater or jacket up over your head, wave your arms, don't back down, make yourself intimidating. But I was completely naked, a glowing pale body of flesh. I had no sweater or jacket. I had nothing but a small flashlight. I was the least intimidating I could be standing helpless in the black night. I was a walking dinner invitation.

I turned back toward the house even though instinct told me that's the direction from which I was being watched. I could have climbed into one of the dead cars parked nearby—that probably would have been the saf-est—but I couldn't stay there all night naked; eventually I'd have to go back. My heart rate quickened. I didn't run but walked faster than when I first ventured out, no longer calling "here kitty, kitty." The air was quiet except for my breathing. When I reached the lawn, the oak trees beside the house's shadowy mass brought a false sense of safety. I figured since I was awake and outside, I'd take advantage of the opportunity and squat on the grass to pee.

As I squatted on the lawn, no longer human-like on two legs but ani-mal-like in a crouch, out of the oak tree I had walked beneath only mo-ments before, less than fifty feet from where I was now squatting, I heard a large four-footed animal landing on the ground. I shined my light in that direction, but fear had slowed my reflexes. The beam sliced through the darkness to find only branches, leaves, a solid trunk. The cougar had already silently moved. I stood, not sure which route to the house was best: the front door? The back? I briskly walked to the house, praying *please don't eat me please don't eat me please don't eat me* even though at that time there had never been a known cougar attack on a human in the state of Oregon, a precedent that would change in 2018 with the first lethal attack of a woman in the Mount Hood National Forest.

When I got inside, I shined the flashlight around the living room. Curled up in a soft, gray ball on the rocking chair next to the door, Lacey slept undisturbed, as Steve did in our bedroom, oblivious to my excursion.

Once in this safe confine, my poor judgment dawned on me. As I had walked the driveway, scanning my flashlight from side to side, I had forgotten that cougars can jump up to twenty feet straight up from a standstill. I never thought to look up into the trees where they take shelter. I imagine this scenario over and over again: the cougar leaping up onto a branch and stealthily hiding in the tree as I exit the house, its intense eyes watching me as I walk directly beneath it, seven, maybe ten, feet below.

What if I had raised that light and seen its sleek muscles poised under tawny fur? What if I had gazed into the glow of its amber eyes?

CRACK MY HEART WIDE OPEN

There are three things you should know. First: I have been suicidal twice in my life—at the age of twelve and again at the age of thirty-six. Second: Although I have never attempted suicide, only flirted with it in extreme ideation, I am a suicide survivor. Third: A fifteen-year-old boy named Sean, the first-born child and only son of a dear friend and Lily's first crush, saved my life. He did this by taking his own.

My introduction to suicide came when I was a child of eight or nine. We often heard sirens wailing a few blocks away from my house, traveling from Highway 101 to El Camino Real and on toward Stanford Hospital. On one particular late summer afternoon, as the neighborhood kids and I played outside, that familiar high-pitched wail whizzed down my street. As soon as the ambulance turned the corner and passed my house, we ran after it. My calloused, bare feet pounded the pavement for four blocks to where the ambulance had stopped at a cube-like, cement-sided, two-story house on Walter Hayes drive. A small crowd of people stood in front of the Pepto-Bismol-pink house, watching two policemen coax a man onto a gurney as paramedics stood nearby. The man wore white boxer shorts and a white cotton undershirt that contrasted with his shiny black skin. There appeared to be a bloody hole the size of a quarter at his throat. He shifted erratically in circles eluding the officers, who stood nearby. "It would be better for everyone if you lie down and cooperate," they said, trying to avoid the use of force.

"What happened?" we whispered.

"He tried to kill himself," we were told. "By cutting his throat and jumping out the second-story window."

Finally, the man lay down on the gurney. He looked at all us kids watching and tried to reassure us, saying "Everything is going to be okay. I'm going to be okay." As he spoke, the red spot on his throat moved, raw and wet. Was he trying to reassure us or himself? The story that circulated through the crowd was that he came from somewhere in Africa to work in the States, and he had tried to bring his family into the country, but they had been denied entry. So he had cut his throat then jumped out the second story window onto the concrete driveway. He then proceeded to roam the neighborhood, assaulting my friend, Raji, who happened to be playing in front of her house, by hitting her over the head with a baseball bat.

The paramedics wheeled the man to the ambulance and loaded him inside. All the while he said, "Don't worry. Everything will be all right." Whom did he see when he stared into our frightened eyes? Was he speaking to his children? I glanced down the street to where a policeman was interviewing Raji's sari-clad mother. Raji was nowhere in sight. If this man missed his children so much, I wondered, why would he hit a child over the head with a bat? Was he mad because other children got to be here when his own could not? I stared up at the small square window, wondering how he fit through the opening, for he was a large man. How did he not hurt himself upon landing? And what made that round hole in his throat? As the paramedics closed the doors of the ambulance, blocking the bloody hole from view and silencing the man's assertions that everything was going to be all right, I glanced once again at the upstairs window. Was the man's suicide attempt spontaneous, the kind without a plan? Is that why he didn't succeed? Or was it a cry for help? As a young child, I did not have an answer, but one thing seemed clear: if he really wanted to commit suicide, he chose a very strange way to go about it.

❂

The photographs from Lily's seventh-grade field trip don't show a teenage boy in turmoil. They show a group of young teens smiling and happy. In the swimming pool. At the campground. Near the Lava Tubes. There is no indication that one week from then one of those faces would be lifeless and the rest of the bright, goofy faces would become tight, crumpled, distressed. Do photos deceive? Or do we see only what we want, subjects putting on a good face? It doesn't matter what you're feeling; here's the expectation: Smile for the camera. On the count of three, everybody say *Cheese*.

A week after the field trip, the phone startled me awake at six in the morning. I clambered out of bed and rushed to stop the ringing before my family woke. *Who is calling so early?* I wondered. When I answered, I heard my friend, Yatiel, say, "I have something to tell you."

Immediately, the groggy fog that was my brain began to clear. "Okay," I said, sitting down on the couch. It's amazing how the mind can move from a state of deep subconscious quiet to confused clutter to rapid awareness all in a few swift beats of the heart, a few ragged breaths.

"Sean is dead," she said. "He killed himself."

Oh my god. No. "How . . . how did he do it?"

"He hung himself. I'm sorry to be the one to tell you," she said. "I got the call late last night. Now I'm notifying people before school starts."

School. What am I going to say to Lily? I thought. *How am I to tell her that the boy she likes, her first real crush, is dead, by his own hand, no less?*

"No," I said loudly. "No!"

And then they were there. My family. Steve, Akela, Lily. They didn't enter the room, just stood in the doorway, staring, disheveled from the abrupt awakening. I stared back. But only one held my gaze. Thirteen-year-old Lily. Her blue-gray eyes, her plump lips, her round cheeks. I knew I was about to break her. My fingers would clutch the paper-thin shell of her heart. I would try not to crush it. But I would fail.

"I have to go," I said to Yatiel and hung up.

I could tell you that when I heard those words, the ground beneath me fell away, like crumbled pavement washed into a raging river. I could also tell you that it was like standing on a beach and watching, paralyzed, as the tide was sucked way out, exposing the sandy ocean floor, and a tower of a wave crested, ready to swallow everything in its path. For that's what it felt like—drowning. Reality shifted. One moment I was asleep. The next I stood naked in my living room, yelling "No!"

The thought of saying the words Yatiel had just spoken, forming the syllables, speaking them out loud to my thirteen-year-old daughter, instilled in me so much panic that there was only one viable option: I tore open the back door, flew down the steps, ran into the yard. My mind wouldn't slow down, wouldn't shut off. All I could think was, *How can this be happening? This can't be happening.*

I paced back and forth, the palm of my hand pressed to my chest, fingers clenching my skin. The jagged rocks of the gravel driveway poked my bare feet, but this did not slow me. I continued pacing, clenching, shaking my head, saying, "No." I glanced through the trees at the neighbors' house several hundred feet away. Could they hear me? Was I being too loud? Had they also gotten a call?

Steve had followed me when I ran from the house. "What happened?" he now asked.

Maybe, I thought, *if I never say it, then it never will have happened.*

I stopped pacing and forced myself to take deliberate breaths. The girls were in the house; I didn't have to say it in front of them.

"Sean's dead," I said. "He hung himself. How can we tell Lily?"

Steve stood there for a moment, still and quiet, hands in his pockets, eyes downcast. Was he hearing me correctly? *How can he just stand there?* I thought. *Doesn't he realize the magnitude of the situation? Can't he freak out like a normal human being?* But everyone's got their own way of processing bad news. Mine was to lose it and become emotionally debilitated. Steve's was pragmatic. In that moment I couldn't accept Steve's reaction. I was too consumed by my own.

"We need to go tell Lily," he said and turned back toward the house.

Both girls sat cross-legged on the couch, silently waiting. Steve told them that Sean was dead.

Lily looked up at Steve. Her eyebrows rose slightly, knitted toward each other. "How did he die?" she asked.

"He killed himself," Steve said.

And then a rush, Lily said, "I didn't think he would really do it. I told him not to. He promised me he wouldn't. I promised I wouldn't tell anybody."

Was *I* hearing correctly? Sean confided in Lily his suicidal thoughts? *My ears must be deceiving me*, I thought. Not only was I experiencing the loss of a dear friend's firstborn child, a boy only fifteen years old, who chose to end his own life, but I was faced with the fact that he had confided in *my* daughter his thoughts of suicide. In that moment, I realized I had failed as a parent. I had never spoken openly with my children about suicide. How could I have had this oversight? I, who only nine months earlier had been suicidal, had never thought to arm my daughter with the knowledge that if someone confides in her his suicidal thoughts, it is *not* a betrayal of his trust to go for help. Lily thought she was holding Sean's confidence, being a good friend. She wanted him to like her, didn't want to alienate him by tattling. But she was young. And naïve. And now she sat on our couch in the early dawn, tears streaming down her face. How was I to remedy my ensuing guilt and feeling of responsibility? In my desire to protect my children from unpleasantness and instead preserve their innocence, I had succumbed to the usual prescription that discussion on the topic remain taboo, something hidden, avoided, ignored. Surely, my lack of forthrightness contributed to Sean's death—if only by not helping to prevent it. Or was my instinct to protect my children really due to my unwillingness to admit that I, their mother, was also susceptible to being the cause of suicide survivors' pain?

I kneeled on my bare haunches, hands limp in my lap, gazing from Lily to Steve to the dirty, stained carpet to the cold woodstove leaking ash to the window streaked with calcium deposits. Tragedy doesn't care how you are dressed—or whether you are dressed at all. It doesn't wait for you to make a fire to relieve the chill or clean the floor. It doesn't care if you can see clearly through the window.

Lily began to cry. "It's all my fault," she said.

"It's not your fault," we told her.

As the parent, I had to be the one to hold things together, so I went to the bedroom and slid into the protective skin of sweatpants and a T-shirt. Then I picked up the phone and dialed the home of Lily's best friend, Heaven. But there was no answer, only an endless drone of rings. I listened, unwilling to put the receiver back on the cradle, unable to accept that the reinforcements I so desperately needed were unavailable. Then a car drove up the driveway. Heaven and her mother, Marie, the very reinforcements I had been calling upon, had arrived.

I suspect Lily had a crush on Sean before going on the class field trip. When I dropped her off at school the morning they were to leave on the trip, it seemed important she ride with her friend, Selene, in her mother's car, a new four-wheel-drive SUV rented specially for the trip. At the time I thought the car was the attraction, not Selene's fifteen-year-old brother Sean, a homeschooler who was going with them. Windows rolled down, the Backstreet Boys blasting, they took off in style as I waved goodbye. It wasn't until they arrived back at school five days later that I learned her motivation. All the cars had arrived except one. When I asked one of the chaperones, "Where's Lily?" she said, "Oh . . . she's with Sean." A simple enough answer. But it was the hesitancy in her voice after that "Oh"—and the tone—that gave it away. Later, it was the photo of the two of them leaving the Lava Tubes that confirmed it. Taken from a distance, it catches them from behind, walking hand in hand up the path in a drizzle.

Sean left no note, no explanation. His actions are left to speculation. This is how I have come to reconcile his death: I will myself to understanding through the belief that Sean suffered intense sadness and hopelessness due to depression. I have no way to confirm this conclusion. I simply believe this because I have felt those things.

I had moments, washing dishes at the kitchen sink, lost in thought, spinning down, down, unable to shut it off—the negativity. Before I learned the power of mindfulness, of becoming aware, of making a conscious choice not to go into the darkness, I just followed the stream of negative thoughts as they swirled in a centrifugal spin, like when the plug in the bathtub is removed, and the gravitational pull sends the water spiraling down, down, with that sucking sound of being swallowed into the pipe. *I am a terrible mother. I am unlovable. I am not deserving of forgiveness. I am a loser. I will never succeed in life.* These thoughts would settle in the pit of my stomach, and I'd stop washing the dishes and crawl beneath the covers, lie there motionless, eyes open to the world but not really seeing. Sometimes, I'd feel heaviness in my heart like layers of wet, coarse wool army blankets sitting on my chest, and with each layer of blankets, the heaviness grew to an intolerable weight, so that I began to suffocate, felt like I was decomposing in a dark, dank hole, my fingernails worn to raw nubs from scratching at the walls of my deepening grave. And my foremost thoughts were of how to end it, how to end the pain, even though standing all around me was beauty—in the way the light filtered through the trees, in the cloud formations in the sky, in my children's round faces and the way their voices spilled from their lips—yet the beauty washed over me and instead of lifting me up, I felt drowned by drinking it in; it filled my lungs, and I could not breathe, it crushed me so. Did Sean feel this too?

Nine months before Sean killed himself, Steve and I were in marriage counseling with therapist number two. On our last visit with this particular therapist, we sat in the rocking chairs that occupied the therapist's tiny, square room. Steve was saying he didn't think our relationship was going to work out; he was ready to give up, move on. We had been through this before—him wanting relief from my anger, feeling that his life consisted of navigating through a mine field, which made him withdraw from the relationship, me frustrated with the lack of love and affection I was receiving, which made me more irritable and combative. This was our dance. Only now, our troubles were compounded by my depression. My fighting nature, the thing that had always ensured my survival, was withering. Honestly, I don't know which came first, the depression or the crumbling marriage. Did my depression begin because Steve wanted to leave me and I feared abandonment? Or did Steve want to leave me because my depression was a manifestation of my own self-concept—that I was unlovable and therefore unworthy. I only know that this time when he said he thought the relationship was over, it felt for real.

The counselor had one elbow on the arm of her chair, her chin resting in her hand. She looked bored. She remained silent, her mouth cast into a frown. Maybe she, along with Steve, thought our relationship was doomed. Or maybe she just didn't have any more tools to offer us. All she did was stare, her legs crossed, the torso of her long body stooped and downcast. *Why is she dejected?* I wondered. *It is my husband who wants to break up, not hers!*

"All right then," I said, "what's the point in being here?"

I got up to leave. The counselor offered no words of advice. She made no attempt to ascertain how I was feeling or if I was a threat to myself. She did not reassure me that even if this were the end of my marriage, it would not be the end of my world. If she had, that type of comment might have seemed trite. But in that moment, all I could feel toward her was resentment for not even trying.

Steve and I silently climbed into our van and headed downtown. I didn't know where we were going. It didn't seem to matter. Nothing mattered. I refused to speak, just watched the landscape roll by. Steve felt bad. But I didn't care. *Let him feel like shit*, I thought.

"Pull over," I said.

He stopped. I got out of the vehicle. We were in town—twenty-five miles from home. I didn't consider this fact. I just started walking. Steve didn't try to stop me. What I didn't know was that he immediately went to a pay phone and called the counselor. He told her of my abrupt exit and asked if he should worry about me hurting myself.

"No," she said, "I don't think she'll hurt herself."

But how could she have been sure?

I headed in the direction of home. I was wearing slipper-like Uggs, and my feet shifted inside them. At first sidewalks lined the highway. But once I got to the edge of town, the sidewalks disappeared, forcing me to walk on the gravel shoulder between the drainage ditch and traffic sailing by at fifty-five miles an hour. I was not sure which was safer, walking with the traffic and not seeing what was coming at me from behind or walking against the traffic and potentially being hit head-on by a car coming around a curve. I opted for going with the traffic. I could have hitchhiked. I had done it before. But I was not in a hurry. I decided to leave it up to chance. Maybe someone I knew would recognize me and offer me a ride. But no one stopped. The cars kept coming in a sporadic, ongoing flux. With each vehicle that passed, a gust of wind wrapped my body and nudged me off kilter, my feet sliding not only in my shoes, but on the loose gravel. The road was relatively straight until I reached the golf course; then the curves began and the shoulder tightened, leaving a paltry three-foot-wide space to walk. So I crossed the highway and trudged up the other side, crisscrossing this way for some time. I don't know how many acres of bucolic farm pastures I passed. But the bright light of day began to cast shadows, and my feet began to tire. As I approached the next small enclave, seven miles from where I started, I wondered what time I would arrive home if I walked the remaining eighteen miles. I imagined it could take all night. My kids would worry. So when I got to the gas station, I used the pay phone. But Yatiel, who commuted to town for work, was unavailable. As I hung up, I noticed a familiar car parked at the gas pump. I walked up to the window and knocked. My friend, Judy, had just picked up her son from school.

"I need a ride home," I told her.

"Climb in," she said.

The next day Yatiel called. "Do you have a plan?" she asked.

"A plan?" I said, confused. *What is she talking about?* Then I understood. She wanted to know if I had a plan for how I was going to kill myself. She knew the procedure. As a licensed clinical social worker who worked with at-risk youth, it was her job to ask this kind of question of anyone she suspected to be at risk, whether they were her clients, or in my case, her friend. I had confided in her my thoughts a few times—not in detail—but she knew enough to be wary. I suppose when her husband relayed the message that I was walking home from town after a bad therapy session, her concern rose to the level of asking this question.

"No, I don't have a plan," I said.

But I had thought about it, many times, many scenarios. I considered pills. This option did not seem foolproof. Chances are someone would have found me and gotten my stomach pumped. Besides, I hate swallowing pills.

I considered shooting myself, but I didn't have a gun and leaving a huge mess for loved ones to clean up was unappealing. However, I could have gone into the woods and shot myself. Nature wouldn't have minded the mess. I considered driving off a cliff or into a tree. But then I would have wrecked our car and left the family without wheels. Not practical.

Do all suicides begin with a plan? Are they stealthily conceived or spontaneous acts? Did Sean have a plan? He had the rope. Was he just waiting for an opportunity? Or had his pain become so acute he couldn't take it anymore, he just wanted it to stop? Right then. Right there. The thing is, when you contemplate suicide, when you really consider it an option, you don't think about the fact that it's a permanent solution to a temporary situation.

It would have been easy to kill myself as I walked home from town—if I had really wanted. All I would have had to do was walk in front of traffic. But it wasn't part of the plan. My walking that seven-mile stretch was a test. I tempted fate to see if I might get hit. I tempted fate to see if I might be saved.

❂

The afternoon I learned of Sean's death, I sat on the lawn in the yard, holding Lily, staring at the evergreen forest, listening to a hum of insects, the breeze punctuated by bird calls and chicken squawks. It was a brilliant, sunny day—aqua blue sky, fertile green awash in every direction. Lily lay in the grass, her upper body in my lap, leaning against my chest. She moved in and out of weeping. I cradled her. That's all I could do—stroke her hair, wrap my arms around her, my hands firm but gentle. Every now and then she spoke half-cracked confessions of guilt and sorrow. And I murmured, "It's not your fault." We sat this way for hours, in this shifted reality where nothing else mattered, rejoined by stillness, the sensation of time stopping. And then we went to the house of another family, our friends, Heidi and Paul and their three kids, and we sat some more.

Surviving suicide is like balancing on the edge of a blade. Either way the knife flashes, you're going to get cut. Certain thoughts kept hacking their way into my consciousness: *What could I have done differently? If only I had reached out more. I should have seen this coming.* I knew the guilt I bore. I could only imagine the guilt Sean's parents must be feeling.

The next day, all the children of the small community charter school gathered in a wide circle in the meadow. Interspersed among them were parents and crisis counselors, coworkers of Yatiel's, to assist with grief counseling. We divided into small groups based on age, with two grief counselors per group. I went with the teens. We sat outside their classroom, on chairs, desks, a couch, the discussion open for anyone to speak. One boy said he didn't understand why Sean did it. A girl revealed that Sean had called her the day before his death and left a message, but she didn't call him back. Sean's sister said she felt abandoned.

Lily raised her hand. She said, "Sean told me stuff."

She said he had shown her scars where he had cut himself. She said he spoke of killing himself, but she made him promise he wouldn't. She said she felt it was her fault because she didn't tell. Hearing these words once again, in the presence of others, fractured me. I could barely look at Lily. Her eyes were red and swollen, her skin pale. I could see the collapse in her chest, the weariness of holding in her emotions. She sat cross-legged on the hard desk, confessing to a large group of people what surely, to her, must have felt like sins. She was being brave. Yet I took the easy way out: escape. *Again.* I got up. This time my hand covered my mouth instead of clutching my chest, in an attempt to stifle my gasps. I walked at first, then ran, through the classroom, out the sliding glass door, into the madrone forest. My knees buckled. Face to the dry, leaf-scattered ground, I sobbed. Later I was told that as I ran away, Lily said, "See, even my mom is mad at me."

✿

What does it take to really want to commit suicide? What does it take to attempt it? Statistics show that in the United States, females attempt suicide 1.4 times more than males, while 3.6 males for every single female complete suicide. A friend of mine once got a call from an out-of-state friend who said she was calling to say "goodbye"; she had taken thirty Xanax and drunk a pint of whiskey and would be dead soon. Now, I question whether this out-of-state friend really wanted to die. She was desperate, yes—desperate enough to tempt fate. She made one phone call. And that was to my friend thousands of miles away. What would have happened if my friend had not answered, if she had been too busy and the call went to voicemail? This woman would have died. My friend *did* answer her phone, did call 911, and was transferred to the dispatch several states away, and the authorities broke into the suicidal woman's house and transported her to the hospital where she was saved. This woman's pain was severe enough that tempting fate must have seemed a rational gamble: either way she'd be relieved from her suffering.

Is there a difference between those who contemplate suicide, those who attempt it but do not succeed, and those who complete it? Maybe there is a certain line, a precipice, if you will, where in the midst of despair, those who are predisposed to complete suicide fall to one side, tumbling down the mountain, hitting rocks and crashing to certain death, while those who are "ideators" or "unsuccessful attempters" fall to the other, only somewhere along the way down, they get caught by a branch or land in a crevice that breaks their fall, and it is painful, but the experience wakes them, scratches into them a glimmer of truth of what it means to be alive, cuts them with the realization that they don't really want to die—that to do so would be devastating to those left behind, and they are then embedded with empathy for others, or maybe just a pure, unadulterated appreciation for breath, for blood, for thought and feeling.

Maybe there is a fundamental difference in the physiology and psychology between those for whom suicide steals into their consciousness and those for whom it does not. Steve has never been suicidal. And I imagine he never will be. He does not experience depression and does not appear to be predisposed to such tendencies. Sometimes I want to believe that my raging emotions that often go unchecked, the same ones that allow me to feel for others, that empathic impulse that flushes through my veins with the whooshing of my heart's valves, is the thing that makes me susceptible to suicide. The capacity to feel is what challenges my life—makes it nearly impossible to sustain when the days are overwrought with difficulty. I want to think that those who kill themselves are the empathic ones who just can't bear the pressure and burst. But now, I am not so sure. After Sean's suicide, I watched the tendrils of grief creep through unsuspecting households, watched as grief wound its way around the survivors, constricting their hearts and squeezing until they cracked wide open, and I wonder, is empathy what holds one tethered to earth? Witnessing the grief of losing Sean was the rope that belayed me down the right side of the mountain. It was the thing that made me care too much about what would happen to my loved ones should I fall down the other side.

I know it's not the same for everyone, but, for me, experiencing the aftermath of a suicide cured me of my suicidal tendencies. Sean saved my life. I am painfully aware of this. There are no trade-offs—a life for a life. There is only the awareness of where I was and where I am going—and how I choose to get there. Gratitude. That's one convoluted emotion I feel now.

One week after the field trip, I was leaving the school grounds, walking to the parking lot. Sean's mother had just arrived and was on her way in. Her other children were with their classmates having portraits taken in the lower meadow. As we greeted one another, I thought about Sean. I thought about Sean and Lily. I wondered where Sean was. I had noticed he wasn't on campus and thought it odd he was not there to get his picture taken. I almost said something. The words waited on my breath, ready to come out: "Where is Sean? Isn't he going to get his picture taken?" But I said nothing but hello, smiled, and kept walking.

In her portrait, Lily sits on a log, a few blades of tall grass in the foreground, a blur of yellows, browns, and greens of meadow grass and wildflowers in the background. She does not know that as the camera records this moment, Sean is at home hanging himself. Her expression is content, her face relaxed. She wears khaki pants and a pale-yellow tank top. One arm is bent, elbow on her knee, as she rests her head, chin in palm. Her hand wraps the side of her cheek. She is suntanned from the previous week's field trip. Her long, straight, dark brown hair is brushed and rests in front of her shoulders. Her blue eyes are bright. Her thick, arched eyebrows curve perfectly, framing the slope of her eyes. She is smiling—not an open-mouthed, toothy smile, but soft, full-lipped, gentle.

Reprieve: Spring

Wet, fleshy Pacific tree frogs rally around our home: electric green frogs with dark stripes painted from nose to eye to shoulder; gray-brown frogs with scattered stripes and spots; pale, lime green frogs with an iridescent copper sheen that shines like an overlay of tissue lamé fabric.

They hang out in their usual haunts, nestled into compact nubs camouflaged on grape leaves or foliage spears of day lilies or at the base of ferns and hostas in the shade garden. They suction-cup their way on the outside of windows, flashing stretchy, pale undersides and rubberized slender toes—gripping, peeling, gripping, peeling their way along the glass. They crawl out from behind the loose shingles of the chicken coop when I press on the door to unlatch it and go in search of eggs. They clutch in rhomboid Spiderman repose, front and back legs askance, anticipating my—and thus their—next move.

As young children, in springtime, my daughters participated in what I like to call The Annual Frog Migration. The girls would wander up above our house to the ditch road that meanders through the forest along a retired irrigation ditch, empty Nancy's yogurt containers in hand, to collect tadpoles and frog eggs from the muddy puddles. They would pour the contents of these quart-sized containers into five-gallon tubs, add algae slime collected from the neighbors' pond for food, and fill them to the rim with fresh water. The milky egg sacks floated, gelatinous and flecked with black specks. The tadpoles wriggled erratically. Over time the jelly-blob egg sacks would melt away and the black specks—hundreds upon hundreds—would grow into larger and larger swimming specks that, along with the other tadpoles, grew tails and eyes and, eventually, legs. The tails soon disappeared, as did the frogs once they could make their way out of the tub.

They float in the dog's water bowl on the porch, spread-eagled and weightless, heads above the surface, infusing the water with essence of frog, then slowly grip the rim of the blue glass and nimbly inch their way out while they believe I am not looking.

They hop into the house through the open sliding-glass door, only to gather stray dust bunnies of dog fur that fuses to their moist skin. When I try to gently remove this unneeded springtime sweater, the frog in hand leaps in a great effort of escape.

They secret themselves away in the clothespin bag hanging on a pine branch, which anchors the clothesline, until I reach inside and scoop a handful of wooden pins and damp, delicate flesh. I extricate the limbs from the pins and then release the tender greenness to the craggy bark of the pine tree.

They hide behind shampoo bottles lined up neatly on the off-kilter weathered board beside our outdoor tub. They cling to the redwood siding, white-washed from faded fifty-year-old primer, of the exterior east wall from which the kitchen window looks out on coral red honeysuckle and whomever happens to be bathing. They linger unannounced on the tub faucet, practicing the art of invisibility, legs tucked underneath their bodies, becoming one with the spout spilling water, and remain for the duration of late-night baths.

They jump onto pant legs when we unfold chairs carried from the glassed-in porch out into the shade of the lawn, a mixture of clover and Kentucky bluegrass. Folding chairs are a frog's favorite. They choose the folds and seams, the spaces within the loops attached to the aluminum framing. I suppose they like the soft padding of the seat. Maybe it gives them comfort, a feeling of safety? They startle as I walk through the grass, leaping out unsuspecting from in front of my bare feet.

When I was a child, my mother and I went to watch my eldest brother's baseball game, which bordered a natural ravine on the Baylands Nature Preserve, a 1,940-acre area of undisturbed marshland. Upon exiting the car, we were greeted by a vibrating chorus of croaking. Thousands of newly hatched frogs occupied nearly every spare inch of ground. We were surrounded by a moving amphibian carpet.

I'd like to say that I had bare feet because I went everywhere in bare feet. But I can't remember if they were already bare or if I simply took off my shoes. Either way, I remember trying to creep my way around and between the damp little creatures on tiptoe, my tiny, agile feet moving deftly, for

I was a dancer and lived a good portion of my time on my toes. I walked slowly, deliberately, step by conscious toe-step, seeking the paved spaces in between the profusion of frogs. My mother went on ahead, trying not to step on them. But there were too many. It was the grandest, most incredible bumper crop of frogs I have ever seen, and to this day, I sometimes wonder, *Did I dream it? Was it real?*

And then I see in my mind's eye a very tall man with jet-black hair, a hooknose, and large feet who was walking down the path to his vehicle that day, stepping sure-footed and unwavering on all those beautiful little creatures—he made no effort to avoid them—and I wonder about the nature of humans' capacity for compassion. A group of frogs is called an army, a title better suited for a group of humans, a species prone to fighting. Humans and armies, both, plow forward with aplomb, undeterred by what they may be stepping on or into.

Frogs have two lives. The first is in the water, where they breathe using gills. They leave this aquatic life for their second one on land, where they breathe using lungs. With their lungs, the frogs around our home in springtime serenade us, day and night, their throaty croaks the tenor to the alto of breeze and soprano of wind chimes.

SEARCHING FOR GWEN

M	A	G	L	A	M	A	N	K	P	O	L	F	N
Y	E	W	F	T	J	M	O	I	W	Q	O	R	C
P	O	E	T	R	Y	U	I	G	Y	U	S	A	O
R	Q	N	D	Y	O	A	T	C	N	V	H	X	N
O	J	C	K	T	R	R	C	D	Z	G	U	B	F
S	E	R	R	I	E	T	I	M	N	U	H	S	L
E	S	A	E	U	G	R	D	R	R	P	E	M	I
H	P	T	K	R	O	A	D	F	E	I	R	G	C
A	A	I	A	G	N	E	A	T	T	E	M	P	T
R	L	V	E	N	V	H	X	I	L	M	N	G	E
R	E	E	W	O	P	E	L	U	S	I	V	E	D
O	R	G	T	C	C	I	N	T	I	M	A	T	E
W	D	I	V	N	B	Z	M	L	Y	R	I	C	H
I	O	E	F	I	N	S	I	D	I	O	U	S	O
N	A	S	S	U	J	H	S	R	E	H	A	B	M
G	Q	S	O	N	L	Y	S	E	U	L	C	Q	E
Z	O	A	L	M	Y	K	I	M	E	M	O	I	R
P	L	Y	A	D	V	E	N	T	U	R	E	S	I
V	H	O	C	H	A	N	G	E	D	L	O	V	E
L	I	F	E	N	O	N	F	I	C	T	I	O	N

GWEN	ADDICTION	AMALGAM
MISSING	RELAPSE	HARROWING
ELUSIVE	ADVENTURES	INCONGRUITY
POSSIBILITIES	TWEAKER	CONFLICTED
TRAUMA	INSIDIOUS	SOLACE
INTIMATE	ATTEMPT	CLUES
DEVOTION	CHANGED	FOUND

1. My friend has disappeared. The search poster says she was last seen on March 2, 2017. The font is a large block print in white on bright red. A warning. Her sweet face looks out from the page. This photo grips me like a fist squeezing my heart when I see the poster the first time. I am reminded of how she used to look—bright blue eyes; smooth, shiny, rosy skin; straight, white teeth, smiling. But this is not the sole cause of my reaction. Neither is the thought that that face could have come to harm. The squeezing heart-grip is because I know this photo. I took it. In my house. She is sitting on my couch, smiling at me through the lens. We were celebrating "Second Thanksgiving" in January when Akela was home from college for winter break four years earlier. What this search poster photo doesn't show is that next to her on the couch sits her six-year-old son. He grins, looking sideways from the camera, toward someone else. His head leans against his mother's arm; her hand rests against his hair.

A couple weeks before this search poster was released, I had received a text from Gwen's sister seeking information and help in finding her. Gwen's family, who live on the east coast, hadn't heard from her for more than two weeks. She wasn't answering her phone, and her voicemail box was full. In an ordinary situation, it could be rationalized that a grown adult might be busy and late in returning calls. But her life is not ordinary. Such rationalizations could not be justified. Her family notified authorities and have since hired a private investigator. She is currently listed as **MISSING**.

2. Some missing people are never found. Some are never found alive. Some people don't want to be found. They hide. From the law, from people they owe money to, from abusive ex-boyfriends. They hide out of fear or shame or because they are out of their minds. They are like smoke sifting through a screen—**ELUSIVE**.

3. My imagination leaps in appalling bounds. Could she have been abducted?

Is she the victim of human trafficking? Did her ex-boyfriend kill her in a drug-induced rage and dispose of her body? Did the stress of losing custody of her son and the havoc of a life destroyed by methamphetamine spur her to suicide? Is she holed up in an abandoned house, alone or with other addicts? Did she suffer a seizure, heart attack, or stroke from overdosing? Is she slipping past us on the rural highway, unsuspected in someone else's rig, close yet unreachable? Or could she be in rehab? The ideal scenario, but not likely. So many **POSSIBILITIES**.

4. Her family flew from Virginia to Oregon to meet with the state police and private investigators. They held a meeting—to share and gather information that may lead to Gwen's whereabouts—outside on an eighty-five-degree day at the community land in our small town. This is the land where my children once attended an alternative school, where I taught cooking, quilting, and crafts, that after much hard work and effort, failed to secure its charter. The land where my missing friend once taught my young daughters belly dancing and a father (of a boy) complained it was irresponsible and improper. The land I walked fourteen years prior as school pictures were being taken on a similar afternoon, yet one not so hot, while Sean was alone at home and hanged himself from a tree. This is the land I normally avoid because it holds memories deep in its soil the way a healed flesh wound holds scar tissue from **TRAUMA**.

5. Here is the nature of my relationship with Gwen: when Akela was in the pediatric intensive care unit at Doernbecher Children's Hospital in Portland, and I was at my most vulnerable because I didn't know if my daughter would live or die, I made one phone call to a friend. She was the one. **INTIMATE**.

6. When Akela was two years old, she used to follow my friend around our property as Gwen worked transplanting, watering, or weeding in our nursery. My daughter's refrain then was, "Only my Gwen." An announcement. A claiming. I know this feeling. I feel it too. No matter how many people love her, no matter how many close relationships she has had, I will always think of her as "only my Gwen." **DEVOTION**.

7. This is what happens when you smoke methamphetamine: it releases an onslaught of dopamine, producing a rush of intense pleasure, followed

by a prolonged sense of euphoria that lasts between six and twelve hours. The amount of dopamine released is twelve times that of activities like sex or ingestion of alcohol or nicotine or certain foods. Dr. Richard Rawson, associate director of UCLA's Integrated Substance Abuse Programs, says, "methamphetamine produces the mother of all dopamine releases." After the drug wears off, depression counters the pleasure and euphoria, inciting repeated use of the drug to avoid turbulent crashes. Such behavior leads to **ADDICTION**.

8. Once, a few years before Gwen disappeared, she called and said, "Will you come get all the alcohol out of my house? I need it out of here. *Now.*" I didn't hesitate. She loaded me up with bottles of hard liquors, liqueurs, wine, and prescription pills not prescribed to her. I promptly placed them in the back of my car. We sat for a long time, discussing her addiction. I said, "Maybe you should go to AA," knowing that if she didn't get help, her newfound sobriety would likely be brief. She balked. "Oh, no. I could never do that," she said. I offered to take her. She said she'd think about it.

A month later, she called. "Hey, Lore, I'd like to get my bar back," she said.

"Your bar?" I said. *What the fuck?* I thought. "I gave it away."

"You gave it away? But I just gave it to you to hold for a little while."

"No, you didn't."

"What about the pills? Do you still have those?"

"No," I said. "I threw them in the garbage."

A few months after that, at her birthday party, she was so drunk, she floated naked in the hot tub, not buoyant above the water, but mostly submerged. Ophelia in the river before she drowned. **RELAPSE**.

9. It wasn't always fractures and chaos. There were times of sweetness and fun. There was the Oregon Country Fair. By day, we sold velvet and lace halter tops, shawls, skirts, and dresses we had designed and sewn together. By night, we roamed the oak-tree paths arm in arm so as not to lose one another. There was the trip to Arcata for her birthday to see Rickie Lee Jones in concert at Humboldt State University. We stopped at the Smith River along the way, stripped off our clothes and plunged into the icy, green water. We lay on our backs bobbing above the rocks, water sluicing over and around our curves until our pale skin turned watermelon from the cold. Later, after the concert, we drove to Patrick's Point, where we had set up a tent on the bluff above the ocean, and climbed into our sleeping bags,

huddling together in the dark, all warmth and closeness, crashing waves and minty breath, as we drifted into sleep. There was a trip to Bandon by the sea, Gwen newly pregnant, me seeking a reprieve from motherhood. When the VW bus we were driving broke down in Winston, rather than canceling our excursion, we left the vehicle at an auto repair shop and rented a car. We stayed at the Sea Star Hostel, ate fish and chips in the sunshine along the wharf with the seagulls, searched for agates on the beach. We trespassed on an abandoned blueberry farm for sale along Highway 1, where the blueberry bushes stood high above our heads, and drove far up Elk River Road until we found the perfect emerald swimming hole down a steep trail, a hidden oasis. A couple years later, there was an overnight at the Greensprings Inn, soaking together in the Jacuzzi tub, singing as she played the guitar, and pulling her son on a sled in the snow the next morning. **ADVENTURES.**

10. I ran into her ex-husband the day Gwen was summoned to an emergency court hearing because he had filed for temporary sole custody of their son. I was out walking with my family at a local nature preserve. Their son was subdued and walked away from us, downcast. He had just learned he would not be seeing his mother for a while. "She's been making poor choices and hanging out with the wrong people," her ex said. "I never would have thought she'd become a tweaker." He did not say she had become a "meth user." In fact, he did not know this as certainty. But everything implied it. The way her once good looks had faded from bright and lively to gaunt and strung out. The way her mood could swing and she'd surge into sudden rage and violence, like the episode that provoked the emergency hearing. The way she couldn't seem to maintain a steady home, work, or previous years-long friendships. "**TWEAKER**" implied meth.

11. Methamphetamine is made from pseudoephedrine (decongestant found in cold medicine) and other highly toxic ingredients, which can include acetone (nail polish remover or paint thinner), lithium (used in batteries), toluene (used in brake fluid), hydrochloric acid (used to make plastic), red phosphorus (found in matchboxes, road flares, and other explosives), sodium hydroxide (lye), sulfuric acid (used in drain and toilet bowl cleaner), and anhydrous ammonia (found in fertilizer and counter top cleaner).

This is what chronic smoking of meth does to a body and brain: The outward physical effects include drastic weight loss, malnutrition, insomnia and sleep deprivation, dental decay, elevated body temperature and dehydration, sores and abscesses, and an aged appearance. The unseen effects can be irreversible damage to major organs such as the heart, lungs, liver, and kidneys. An overdose of meth can cause convulsions, heart attack, stroke, or death. Methamphetamine is a central nervous system stimulant that is neurotoxic. Chronic meth use damages the brain and causes chemical changes. Effects include: psychotic symptoms, including paranoia, hallucinations, delusions, and self-absorption; aggression and violence due to a lack of impulse control; impaired thinking and judgment; memory loss; decreased attention span; anxiety; mood swings; reduced inhibition; compulsive motor actions like twitching or scratching; and an increased risk of stroke and Parkinson's disease.

Many words describe how meth affects a life. But there is one word—its signature—that describes best what it is at its core: INSIDIOUS.

12. Her Facebook posts turned dark and desperate, describing in text with pictures how her on-again, off-again boyfriend had trashed her rental and her car. One day, after she had been evicted and was living out of her car and a string of motels (when she could afford it), her rambling post read like a suicide note, addressed to her son as a goodbye letter, saying how tired she was and she just needed to close her eyes and dream of her son in a peaceful sleep. Alarm bells rang in my brain. I immediately called her phone but got no answer, so I messaged her on Facebook, pleading for a response, then I started calling motels. The first motel I called wouldn't confirm if she was staying there. Against policy. I began asking every clerk I called for her room, and when they asked me for the room number, I feigned ignorance. They all came back saying there was no one by that name at their motel. That's when I called the sheriff, but without knowing her location, there was nothing they could do. About an hour later, she messaged me back, telling me where to find her, adding "Please don't send the cops here."

She answered the motel door in a tank top and underwear, her hair stringy and hanging in her face, which looked ashen and haggard with dark patches under her eyes and an expression of both shame and relief at seeing me. The room was freezing because the air conditioner blasted on high, and the air smelled of an unfamiliar toxic chemical I could barely stand to breathe. I pulled a chair close to the bed to face her and said, "I'm here to help you, but you have to be honest with me. If you're not, I'll know it, and I'm outta here."

I quizzed her, and she confessed to everything: using meth for nearly two years, how and when she started, having smoked it prior to my arrival, as well as prior to writing her distressing Facebook post. She said she couldn't keep track of time. Not in the way regular people lose track and are late to an appointment, but in the way time shape shifted so that she wasn't sure what was actual and what was imagined. Whole chunks of time disappeared, and she didn't know what had happened. She warned me she could "go from zero to a hundred" in an instant—one moment she'd be fine; the next she'd be enraged. And then she described an episode (one I had already heard about from another person's perspective) with such clarity and accuracy (and conflicting with the other person's account) that I felt certain she was fabricating the facts. Not lying directly. I think she truly believed what she was saying. It was more like her fabrication was the product of delusion. I expressed no doubt. This was a reconnaissance mission. My intention was to save her, not alienate her. **ATTEMPT.**

13. We went out for dinner at the G Street Bar & Grill. She was in good spirits and mostly acted like her normal self (although an extremely hyped-up version), but as the evening passed, there was an obvious lack of balanced relating. It felt like she could *hear* my voice but wasn't really *listening* to what I had to say. She showed no interest in the changes in my life since we had last seen each other sixteen months before. After dinner, we sat in the car in the parking lot, and a family walked by, a baby sitting on the man's shoulders. I said, "You know I'm a grandma now." She made no remark other than an insulting joke I can't remember now and then started talking about something else. One might think she didn't want to talk about grandchildren because losing custody of her son was too painful. Maybe some of that floated beneath the surface. Her behavior, though, didn't express that much care, thought, or reflection. It revealed dissonance between the person I used to know and the one sitting beside me. That was the defining moment. I realized my old friend was gone. In her place sat a dysfunctional woman who had lost the ability to reason and care about others. By the time we got back to the motel, she was growing confused, agitated, and angry. I left her in the parking lot, searching through the back of her car, muttering to herself in an incoherent repetition, an edge of violence rising in her body. A person **CHANGED.**

14. The vernacular used to refer to addiction and those who struggle with it

has changed. Terms such as "meth addict" and "substance abuser" have become "person with a meth [or substance] use disorder." Such terminology is believed to be person-centered and avoids characterizing one by his or her addiction. The transition away from substance "abuse" is meant to abate the negative moral judgments associated with the word. At the meeting on the community land with Gwen's family, her sister reminded everyone that the last couple of years of Gwen's struggle is only a blip in the timeline of her life. We, who have known her for longer than two years, know the essence of her being—devoted mother; talented musician and belly dancer; healing and intuitive massage therapist; pirate radio DJ, spinning Bluegrass Tendencies; loving sister, daughter, and friend. A person is not one thing or another—addict or responsible adult—she is an AMALGAM.

15. I said I would be her touchstone; she could call me when she needed grounding. I would help her focus, come up with strategies for recovery, and (hopefully) implement them. She called, agitated and struggling to make a to-do list. She couldn't think straight. She couldn't remember what she needed to write down. She said, "just hearing the sound of your voice helps." "Do you want me to come?" I asked. "Yes," she said.

When I arrived, she was on the phone with an insurance representative, trying to get approval for detox. She put the phone on speaker so I could listen. The woman expressed concern that if she went to detox without a bed waiting for her in a rehab center directly afterward, she would relapse and detox would have been futile. Gwen tried to remain calm. Her sole focus was the upcoming custody hearing. She wanted to show the court she was taking steps to get clean. But the insurance rep wouldn't authorize approval, and this agitated Gwen, who had barely slept and not eaten since the day before. I started writing a to-do list for her—get an evaluation from Options (the local nonprofit providing psychosocial rehab services), find a lawyer, get a new phone charger—when a Domino's delivery guy knocked on the door. Gwen's sister had called in a delivery order in hopes she would finally eat. The insurance phone call had stressed Gwen out, and she could barely hold the sandwich still because she was shaking so much. She bit into it aggressively. After one bite, she started a pattern of repeated muttering, like the night before. She babbled about needing her son, about wishing her abusive ex-boyfriend were there—if only she could see him and talk to him, everything would be better.

"Well, you can forget that. He's the last thing you need."

I had said the *wrong* thing. A deep, guttural roar erupted out of her. She rose out of her chair and slammed her fists down hard on the table, inches from where I sat. It rocked from the force. She paced back and forth, tensing her fists, her arms, unadulterated rage hijacking her body. I have been in the presence of rage before. But this rage exploded in unmatched fury and vibrated at a frequency entirely unpredictable. Suddenly I was vibrating too. But with fear. I felt certain she was going to attack me. Then she ran to the bathroom and shut herself inside, yelling in a rush, "Lore, you need to leave, you need to leave, I need you to leave, get out of here, you better get out of here, I need you to get out of here, Lore, now, go, get out of here!" I grabbed my bag and fled. I flew down the stairs, running for what felt like my life, afraid the colossal form of Lyssa, goddess of fury and madness, would swoop into the stairwell and strike me down. **HARROWING**.

16. As I drove home from the motel, past the lush, spring-green farms and fields, it was hard to reconcile the fact that here, in this place teeming with beauty and life and potential, lurked a pathology of people in drug-addled discord, an energy so harmful and frightening it hid amid the grass like a viper waiting to strike. **INCONGRUITY**.

17. Gwen's ex-husband's lawyer called and asked if I would testify against her in court. Until I revealed that Gwen had confessed her meth use to me, they had no confirmation of her addiction, only suspicion and hearsay. The lawyer said my testimony would ensure "court ordered" treatment and put Gwen at the top of a substantial list for in-patient treatment. In Oregon, public rehab centers are maxed out. The wait is long. For a person suffering from methamphetamine addiction, such a wait can feel like a lifetime. A lifetime of continued damage to the brain and body. The lawyer said the goal was to get Gwen treatment so she could return to being an active part of her son's life with shared custody. She laid out the protocol: detox; ninety-day, in-patient rehab; and then a transition to a halfway house, where she would have support and therapy to reintegrate into living independently a life free of meth. During treatment, she could have access to her son, at first via phone calls and then in person. Court was in a week. I had to make a choice. Would I sacrifice our relationship to help save her life? *Yes, absolutely*, I thought. *Maybe someday she'd forgive me.* Even Gwen's sister supported me in testifying. But then I thought about Gwen's fragile state, the delicate trust she had instilled in me, how she had said, "You're my only

friend who isn't a drug addict," and I wasn't sure if I could do it. With my testimony, the temporary full-custody order in favor of Gwen's ex would become permanent. She'd hate me for that. **CONFLICTED**.

18. Gwen found a lawyer who took her case pro bono, and they settled out of court. She signed an agreement requiring her to get treatment, just as her ex's lawyer had described, and I was relieved of making the decision of whether to betray her. She never went to in-patient rehab. I could have testified against her, and it still wouldn't have ensured her recovery. It most likely would have ruined our friendship though. The last time I saw her she was evicting me from her motel room. It was tense and terrifying and un-predictable. But I knew she loved me. There is that, a bit of **SOLACE**.

19. When Gwen went missing, her last phone call was to a friend on the East Coast. For Gwen, her phone was her lifeline. She remained tethered to it—until she lost it. She lost multiple phones in the last year leading up to her disappearance. Every time she lost one, she contacted her sister, who paid the phone bill, to get a replacement. After that last phone call, Gwen didn't seek a new phone. The voicemail box filled up, and her family was no longer able to reach her. There were no sightings of Gwen or her car. Three months later, after her family hired a private investigator and the Oregon State Police agreed to take the case, Gwen's car was found in the north end of Grants Pass, behind some motels adjacent to Interstate 5. Authorities reviewed security footage, but the cameras record over old footage every week or so, so they came up with no new leads. I heard rumor that the contents of her vehicle included her phone, laptop, and a tablet. All evidence remains in police custody. Her family continues to ask for prayers and everyone to "keep the faith" in hopes this information will help find her. **CLUES**.

20. To deal with the fact that Gwen is missing, I have developed a numb-ness of spirit in her regard. I cannot linger too deeply in the questions of who, what, where, when, why, and how, for if I do, a sinking dread threatens to bury me. Sometimes it does. Temporarily. But then I squash it back into numbness. Numbness allows hope to thrive. That hope is a seedling that roots itself in a crack of concrete, defying heat, drought, and the soles of shoes in order to grow. This essay is my invocation. It calls on the miss-ing and transforms her from elusive smoke sifting through a screen to

something tangible. I wonder how Gwen might react to it. Gwen the addict would probably go nuts and rail against my words, positioning herself as the victim, blaming me for betraying her confidence and accusing me of an inaccurate portrayal. Gwen the person and friend not addicted to meth might feel some shame. Maybe some regret. Perhaps she would see her story as the story of a thousand others. Perhaps in reading this essay, she would be thankful to have lived through the story and come out the other side. I'm willing to take that gamble. I'm willing to risk her hating me. That would mean I'd see her again one day. That would mean she will be **FOUND**.

ANSWER KEY:

M	A	G	L	A	M	A	N					F	
	W			M	O				O		C		
	E			U	I		U			O			
	N		Y	A	T		N			N			
			T	R	C	D				F			
	E		R	I	T	I			S	L			
	S		E	U		D		E	I				
H	P		K	R		D	I		C				
A	A		A	G	E	A	T	T	E	M	P	T	
R	L		E	N	V	I		E					
R	E		W	O	E	L	U	S	I	V	E	D	
O	R		T	C	I	N	T	I	M	A	T	E	
W			N	B	M								
I	O		I	N	S	I	D	I	O	U	S		
N			S		S								
G		S	O		S	E	U	L	C				
	O		L		I								
P		A	D	V	E	N	T	U	R	E	S		
		C	H	A	N	G	E	D					
		E											

BAD BLOOD

I.

The eighth-floor corridor of Doernbecher Children's Hospital at Oregon Health Sciences University is silent except for my hurried footsteps. It's been a couple hours since I boarded the commercial flight from Medford to Portland then hired a taxi to get here. Akela has been transported by Mercy Flights for emergency exploratory abdominal surgery. With each footfall, I think, *I hope I am not too late.*

When I reach the sign, PEDIATRIC INTENSIVE CARE UNIT, I turn left and pass through a short, L-shaped hallway that ends at double doors. The reception station is empty. I ignore the sign that reads "Please check in before entering" and push through the swinging doors.

The unit is quiet—except for one corner room to the left illuminated by glaring lights. Several nurses in scrubs and a small man in a knee-length white coat are positioning Akela's hospital bed and hooking her up to monitors. I am vaguely aware that Steve stands nearby, but I don't pay attention to him; my focus is on Akela, lying still and unresponsive. They have arrived only minutes before me.

"Here comes Mom," one of the nurses says.

I stride toward the open, sterile room, a three-sided cubicle with a heavy vinyl curtain shoved to one side like a compressed accordion. I drop my overstuffed duffel bag onto the tile floor. Two of the nurses and the doctor surround me. "When did she first become ill? What were the symptoms? Did she suffer any type of fall?"

They guide me to reveal every detail of the past few days: abdominal pain, nausea, vomiting, fever, improvement then worsening. I have recited the same litany numerous times in the last nine hours. I look over my shoulder at the delicate frame in the hospital bed. Akela lies there, face slackened and sallow, dimples undetectable. The doctor and nurses don't know that she has deep dimples; right now, her most distinct facial feature remains a secret.

"We can't tell what is going on in there," the doctor says.

I gaze slightly down at him, for he is several inches shorter than me—and I am only four feet eleven. *A miniature doctor for miniature people*, I think.

"The CT scan shows an excess of fluid in her abdomen, evidence something has ruptured," he says, "but we won't know until we open her up. The possibilities are a ruptured appendix, bowel, or stomach. The appendix would be the best-case scenario."

After the doctor has explained the potential remedies, two of the nurses corral me to the side of the room, consent forms in their hands. I need to sign permission for the surgery and medications. I scrawl my name across every line marked with an X. One of the nurses then presents another form and says, "This is for permission to give her blood products. She may need a transfusion, and the doctor wants to give her platelets before the surgery to ensure she won't have trouble clotting."

I freeze, pen in hand, instilled with panic. All I can think of is this: Contaminated blood. Communicable diseases. AIDS. It's not rational. Standardized national testing for HIV in the nation's donated blood supply was implemented in 1992, with the first HIV screening tests beginning in 1985. So at this time, February 2007, the chance of contracting HIV through a blood transfusion is one in two million, comparable to the chance of getting struck by lightning. Still, when I am presented with the simple task of signing my name to allow Akela to be given blood products, the thought that pervades my mind is *What if I sign the consent and they give her contaminated blood and I have signed an execution warrant for my child?*

An execution warrant—that is a pretty extreme viewpoint for a scenario that runs a one in two million risk. But in this moment, I don't know what the risk is of contracting HIV through a blood transfusion. I don't know what the risk is of contracting hepatitis C, or hepatitis B, or variant Creutzfeldt-Jakob disease, or any other blood-transmissible disease. I only know the fear I feel. Fear of contamination.

✺

As I pulled into the gravel parking lot of our small-town post office on a lazy spring day in 1996, a large woman around the age of sixty was getting out of my friend Craig's Toyota minivan. Although I hadn't seen Craig in a couple months, I knew he was at home, ill with walking pneumonia, a condition that evolved from a bad case of bronchitis. Curious, I stopped to investigate by saying hello and introducing myself. The woman told me she was Craig's wife. I paused, quite taken aback. In the last two months since Craig first became ill, he had contracted more than walking pneumonia; he had contracted a wife—a wife he had never mentioned in all seven years of my knowing him. I scrutinized this new wife, her overlarge breasts that curved with the weight of the rest of her heavy build, her lined face, her gray hair that nearly reached her rump. She looked close to twenty years older than Craig. Not the type of woman I imagined my handsome, eccentric, entrepreneur friend to marry. His last known girlfriend, seven years earlier, had been an innocent twenty-one-year-old. *Who is this woman? And where did she come from*? I wondered.

Once home, I told Steve, "You're never going to believe this. Craig has a wife!"

"A wife?"

"Yeah, I met her at the post office. She said that Jim, the postman, picked her up from the airport and acted as the witness at the ceremony. They got married there, on Craig's land. Isn't that weird? I wonder why he didn't call us? Why would he call Jim instead of us?"

Over the next few months, Craig's condition continued to worsen. His wife told us the doctors couldn't figure out what was wrong; they'd done test after test to no avail. One day, Steve came home from visiting Craig and burst through our back door, blue eyes glistening with tears, sudden gasps of air escaping his lungs. "Craig has AIDS," he said, grabbing me, hugging tight, his body shuddering against mine.

Steve described how he had sat next to bed-ridden Craig and told him, "I'm going to figure out what's wrong with you. I'll do whatever it takes. We'll find a cure."

The wife's grown daughter from a previous marriage had overheard Steve and confronted her mother, telling her, "You've got to tell him. You can't let this guy go on worrying like this."

❂

In 1987, Steve's oldest sister Kathy died of stomach cancer the morning after Thanksgiving. A year earlier, Steve had volunteered to donate blood prior to the surgery that revealed Kathy's diagnosis because they were the same blood type: A negative. However, the hospital rejected Steve's blood. It showed "signs of possible liver damage." Steve thought the harm to his liver resulted from contact with chemicals and heavy metals while working as an auto mechanic. He had no insurance at the time, so he didn't follow up with a doctor. Instead, from then on, he made an effort to work outside for better ventilation and tried not to touch used motor oil. Steve was thirty-three years old. Hepatitis C virus (HCV) would not be identified by science for another three years, the same year we would meet a hyper-health-conscious, wheat-grass-juice-drinking Craig and move into the upstairs apartment in his house, readying a nest for the birth of our firstborn daughter.

Thirteen years after the identification of HCV, on a sunny day in 2002, Steve will say in a serious tone, "I think I'm going to die." He'd been experiencing extreme fatigue, ringing in his ears, headaches. But because he looked basically healthy, despite the fact that he spent hours in bed due to his fatigue, and because I didn't want to consider that there could *actually* be something seriously wrong with him, I chose to interpret his words as melodramatic rather than intuitive, and I thought to myself, *Well, yes, you're going to die. At some point, we are all going to die.*

Steve made an appointment with a doctor. They drew blood, ran tests. The result: hepatitis C, liver disease. The doctor referred him to gastroenterology. Now that he had been diagnosed with a strictly blood-transmissible disease, questions loomed: How did he get it? And how long had he had it? Steve felt sure he could pinpoint the instance of transmission. At the age of fourteen, he shared a needle with a friend who had a drug habit—the first and only time Steve ever shot drugs. At the time of diagnosis, Steve was forty-nine years old. He had most likely been infected with hepatitis C for thirty-five years, nearly three-quarters of his life.

It only takes one exposure, one needle prick, one droplet of blood.

And that is why when I stand rigid in the PICU five years later, pen in hand, nurses waiting for me to sign consent to give my daughter blood, I hesitate. It's only a moment's hesitation, but long enough for me to become painfully aware that I appear to be a crackpot, ignorant mom for daring to question, in the midst of an emergency, whether I will allow doctors to give my child blood in order to save her life.

Bad Blood. That's what comes to mind when they say the plan is to give her platelets as insurance.

"If it were *my* child, I'd give her the blood," says one of the nurses.

Of course I don't want my child to die. But if that bag of blood is contaminated, would I rather risk saving her life now only for her to be given a disease which at worst could be an early death warrant and at best would assign her to a life of disease management? It's only a moment's hesitation—the amount of time it takes to drop a pen and have it land on the floor. But within this span of hesitation, I realize I have to chance it; Akela has been flown three hundred miles to identify the source of her abdominal rupture and repair it in order to save her life, not let her die on the operating table.

I sign my name.

II.

There are six unique varieties of hepatitis, each differentiated by a capital letter: A, B, C, D, E, and G. Each virus has its own symptoms, severity, and means of transmission. "Hepatitis simply means inflammation, or irritation, and enlargement of the liver," states *The Hepatitis Workbook: A Guide to Living with Chronic Hepatitis B and C.* Steve received this handbook in the mail after his diagnosis, along with a video courtesy of Schering Hepatitis Innovations. One chapter says, "The biggest differences between the hepatitis B and C viruses are in some of the ways they are spread . . . whether they become chronic, and in the way the hepatitis C virus mutates, or changes. . . . Both the hepatitis B and C viruses mutate in the body, but the hepatitis C virus does this so many times that the body ends up fighting many slightly different forms (called strains) of the virus."

I watched the video repeatedly, listening to testimonials of hepatitis C sufferers who relate the shock they experienced upon learning of their condition: the nurse who got jabbed by a needle while taking out the trash after surgery, the man who got a blood transfusion after a motorcycle accident, the mother who nearly died when she hemorrhaged after giving birth. Some don't know how or when they contracted the virus. "How did you get it?" That's the first thing people ask when Steve tells them he has been diagnosed with hepatitis C. I suppose their thoughts flit as fast as it takes to inject a needle into an arm.

Drugs. Needles. Sex. Bad Blood.

It's a chain reaction when one considers possible means of transmission, these thoughts flashing like neurons traveling the pathways to ignite parts of one's brain.

Hepatitis C is spread strictly through blood, mostly via transfusions before July 1992 (when testing became available) and contaminated needles shared by intravenous drug users. While it is less likely nowadays to contract HCV in a tattoo facility than it was before the addition of autoclaves and standard precautions, the results of a multinational study published in the *International Journal of Infectious Diseases* in 2010 reports that among non-intravenous drug users, tattoo recipients are nearly six times more likely than their tattoo-free peers to have HCV. Hepatitis C can also be spread through sharing a toothbrush, razor, nail clipper, or earrings.

Steve and I had shared a toothbrush at one time or another. Had I contracted the virus as the bristles massaged my gums and made them bleed?

Sometime after Steve's diagnosis, I went to a community health center in town for a checkup and was seen by a physician's assistant. The PA asked me a multitude of routine questions, and somehow I found myself telling him that my partner had been diagnosed with hepatitis C.

"Are you still having sexual intercourse with him?" he asked.

"Yes."

"Do you use a condom?"

"No. I was told the chance of getting it through sex is really low."

"Yeah, well, a low chance is still a chance. Is that something you want to risk?"

I sat on the examination bench feeling perplexed and not sure how to respond. I hadn't anticipated this type of question. But before I could answer, he was walking out the door, saying over his shoulder, "If I were you, I'd stop having sex."

Had this man really just suggested I never again have sex with my husband? What does he think? That I'm either going to become abstinent for the rest of my life or find a new partner? According to *The Hepatitis Workbook*, "Most people in a long-term relationship with only one partner seem to be at low risk of spreading or catching hepatitis C through sex."

All the literature I consulted said it is extremely rare for hepatitis C to be passed through sex, unlike hepatitis B, which spreads through bodily fluids—semen, saliva, mucous, vaginal excretions—as well as blood, much like HIV. In fact, the results of a ten-year study on 895 monogamous heterosexual partners suggest that the risk of sexual transmission of hepatitis

C between monogamous heterosexual couples could be null. Despite these findings published in the *American Journal of Gastroenterology*, I was advised otherwise by this health care professional. His proclamation to stop having sex with my husband was based not in scientific fact, but in fear and ignorance. Besides, shouldn't he be advocating the practice of safe sex rather than no sex at all? Still, no matter how much I doubted his knowledge and credentials to be giving such offhand advice, I could not ignore the question it raised. When it comes to taking risks, how low of a risk is low? And why was it that the suggestion to discontinue having sex with my husband due to a very low risk of contracting HCV felt baseless and ignorant whereas the very low risk of my daughter contracting a blood-transmissible disease through a transfusion gave me pause?

❂

Craig's wife left for a month to sell his wares—faceted lead crystals and pewter trinkets—under a large circus-style tent. She placed Craig in a local residential clinic for AIDS patients. She told me the name but not where it was. I searched the phone book, but there was no listing. Determined to visit him, I made calls, asking for referrals. Finally, I reached the clinic. I told the nice man on the line, "I am trying to find my friend so I can visit him."

But he said he couldn't confirm if Craig was a patient. And he wouldn't give me the address or even the general vicinity of its location. "All that information is private."

More like secret, I thought. "I just want to visit my friend," I said. "Bring him some flowers, maybe read to him. Let him know he's not forgotten."

"I'm sorry," the man said. "I wish I could tell you, but because of the nature of the illness, we need to protect the identity of the patients."

I hung up, frustrated. And I wondered about this disease that induced those who suffered it to hide like battered women in a shelter, seeking relief from their abusers. Maybe the HIV patients at this clinic were not hiding. But if not, then *why is there so much secrecy*? I wondered. At that time, I was too immersed in my own thwarted desire to visit Craig to think about the prejudice against people infected with AIDS. Instead I thought, *I am merely a friend offering kindness, compassion*, which then led me to question: does the stigma of AIDS turn the non-HIV-infected world into such a threat? It wouldn't be until years later when I'd realize that in the milieu of 1996, the answer was yes; knowledge of an HIV-infected person's status could threaten insurance, a job, friendships, and more. But at the time, I was dismayed by this secrecy and thought, *Wouldn't those who misunderstand the disease rather keep their distance for fear of catching it?*

❁

When I was in the third grade, I picked at a scab on my knee, squeezing my flesh to get the blood to flow as my friend Marnie worked on a scab of her own. We sat next to the red and white octagonal sign on the corner of Alester and Hamilton Avenues. STOP, it warned. The concrete was rough and scratchy on my bare legs. The smell of freshly cut grass and fertilizer wafted in the breeze. School had let out awhile before. The rest of the children had already gone home. Our intention: to become blood sisters. Dark red droplets came to the surface, and we pressed our limbs together, wound to wound.

In 1974 there was little to no risk of AIDS; it had not yet been identified or begun to spread. No one was yet aware that simian immunodeficiency virus (SIV), the precursor to HIV, flowed through the veins of monkeys and had for nearly thirty-two thousand years. Was there a risk of hepatitis? Yes. But Marnie and I didn't know this, and even if we had, we were too young to care and the likelihood of being infected was null. As I participated in this archaic ritual, Steve had probably already contracted hepatitis C. He was moving through his life with the virus circulating undetected through his veins and arteries.

Red blood cells live an average of 120 days within the body. Like skin, which renews itself, sloughing off and falling away, red blood cells are recycled into a new supply. Platelets form from cells in bone marrow. They have an average life span of eight to twelve days until they are absorbed by the spleen. When given platelets from someone else's body, does the recipient then become a temporary relative of the donor? The definition of a blood relative is one related by blood or origin, especially sharing an ancestor with another. But if the origin is not shared, only the blood, even if only for a matter of days, what does that make donors and recipients? Transitory brothers and sisters bound by our most valuable commodity, the circulatory crimson life force?

❁

Steve and I follow as Akela's hospital bed is wheeled from the PICU to the operating room. Before passing through the double doors into the corridor where we are not allowed, the orderly delivering her into surgery stops so we can say goodbye. I lay my hand on her, lean down, and say, "I love you, honey pie. Everything's going to be all right. We'll be waiting for you when you come back, okay?"

But Steve gently whispers, "She can't hear you. She's already under."

"Oh," I say, melting into weary smallness as Akela disappears through the doors and down the hall. Still, I need to believe that as I spoke to her, before she drifted away from me, she could hear my words, that they were not wasted on empty air.

When Akela returns to the PICU, the surgeon tells us it was a ruptured appendix. They did the best they could to clean out her abdomen of the two liters of pus proliferating inside, but she has a raging systemic infection and runs the risk of developing abscesses.

I don't recall the first time sepsis is mentioned. A word I have never heard until Akela resides in the PICU. The doctors must have said it when they told us the results of her surgery. Sepsis is a potentially deadly response the body develops to an infection. The infection can be bacterial, viral, parasitic, or fungal. Sepsis begins when the immune system releases chemicals into the bloodstream to fight the initial infection, which produces inflammation, but the inflammation does not stay localized to the original point of infection (in Akela's case, the abdomen), and instead a systemic inflammatory response spreads through the entire body. As a result of this pervasive inflammation, microscopic clots form in the blood vessels. The exaggerated inflammatory response impedes the body from being able to break down the clots. The result: the clots prevent organs from receiving and utilizing enough oxygen, causing them to fail.

Usually the very young and the very old are at risk, as are those with compromised immune systems, such as AIDS patients. As of 2020, the Centers for Disease Control and Prevention (CDC) estimated that "Nearly 270,000 Americans die as a result of sepsis" every year and "1 in 3 patients who dies in a hospital has sepsis."

III.

The night before Craig's death, he lay in bed in the center of his living room, a ghostly body hidden under a white sheet pulled up to his chin, his once clean-shaven face now heavy with thick, dark beard and mustache woven with gray. His wife had stopped using a razor on him. She said there was too much risk. She was already in contact with his excrement due to his incontinence; she figured there was no need to increase her exposure. Craig's eyes were closed, but I could see his eyeballs moving, like sparks of static electricity behind his lids. Lamplight from the corner cascaded an eerie yellow glow.

The last time Steve and I visited Craig, he lay in this very same bed, in this very same spot, eyes open, unspeaking, without turning his head to look at us as we sat on short stools in front of the large picture window overlooking the valley. "Your friends are here to visit you, Craig," his wife said. But he wouldn't acknowledge us. Maybe he felt embarrassed by his bed-ridden inability to control his bowels. Maybe he was pissed off (as I imagine someone close to death might be) that everyone around him was thriving while he was deteriorating. Or maybe he had lost his ability to speak. Whatever the reason, we conversed with his wife, her daughter, and son-in-law in front of him, a casual conversation that seemed unfitting for a visit to a dying friend. I suppose normalcy is required in the presence of one who is determined to deny his fate. But it was awkward carrying on this conversation as if he weren't even there.

At one point I had to pee, so I went to use the bathroom. I was nervous going in, lifting the lid of the toilet gingerly, placing toilet paper on the seat. I imagined microbes of the virus lingering unseen on the surfaces—the toilet, the sink, the shower. I knew this to be irrational. HIV lives in concentrations of blood, semen, vaginal fluid, breast milk, saliva, and tears, not on the surfaces of toilet seats or sink faucets. It's rare for the virus to be spread through means other than sexual contact with an infected person or the sharing of contaminated needles or blood products. As I stood in Craig's bathroom, though, fear got the better of me. Was AIDS the culprit behind my irrational thoughts? Had my friend been dying of cancer, I would not have felt squeamish. Was it because, like many, I feared what I did not understand? Watching Craig decline into bedridden incapacitation from a communicable disease sent my ability to be rational down the toilet with the paper I used to wipe my ass. It was the contemplation of exposure. It was the idea that the person lying in the bed in the other room, wearing Depends because he couldn't control his bowels, could be me.

At the end of our visit, when we prepared to leave, I approached Craig's bedside, placed my hand on his, smiled, and said "It's good to see you, Craig." At the time, I believed I had good intentions. But I was a fraud. And I think he knew it. Amidst my nervousness at being in the house and carrying on a trivial conversation within Craig's presence while having no direct interaction with him, I attempted to remedy the situation by imitating his wife's daughter. When she entered the room not long after we had arrived, she went straight to Craig's bed, placed her hand atop his covers, smiled, and said hello. Watching her simple action, I felt ashamed that I hadn't done the same upon my own arrival. Instead, I let myself be ruled by awkwardness and discomfort. And as I exhibited this false portrayal, which surely stemmed from my own need to redeem myself, those blue eyes of his that had always been clear and vibrant now looked dark as dank pond water. And when they met mine, they pierced me with unrelenting intensity—a combination of terror and hatred that clenched my insides and still haunts me.

How could I have been so ignorant? Those words I spoke, "It's good to see you, Craig," they betrayed what was left unspoken: *I'm sorry to see you like this, Craig, debilitated by a harsh disease I don't understand, and I fear you will never get better.* It's no wonder he had that look in his eyes.

So as I looked at Craig on the night before his death, I felt relieved those eyes were closed and could not chill me with that penetrating stare. Steve and I knelt at his bedside, wrapped our arms around him, and lay our heads on his frail body. "We love you, Craig," we said.

Sometimes only at the threshold of death do we act so freely.

As we were leaving the house, I glanced back toward the living room and noticed that as Craig's wife changed his brief, she wore no gloves.

✿

The nurse practitioner in the gastroenterology department requested I join Steve to discuss his treatment options. We waited in the sterile patient observation room until she entered, a woman in her mid-fifties. She sat on the rolling doctor's stool, clipboard and pen in hand. I couldn't help but notice the gargantuan diamond rings on her fingers—gleaming, faceted hunks of rock candy. These status markers were distracting, and, to me, a woman whose husband was here courtesy of the Oregon Health Plan, they also felt inappropriate.

She explained the currently available therapy: REBETRON combination therapy containing ribavirin capsules and interferon injections. The therapy entailed either a twenty-four- or forty-eight-week regimen of taking the capsules three times a day and injections three times a week. The potential prognosis: 40 percent chance of reducing the hepatitis C virus in the blood to undetectable. The side effects: fatigue, flu-like symptoms, muscle pain, loss of appetite, nausea, diarrhea, mild hair loss, anxiety, irritability.

She said, "Some patients experience severe mood swings, personality shifts, and psychiatric episodes including depression, psychosis, aggressive and violent behavior, suicidal ideation, suicidal attempts, and suicide completions." She recited these side effects like the voice over at the end of a prescription drug commercial.

My anxiety rose. *Uh oh, this doesn't sound promising.*

"In rare instances, patients have even experienced homicidal tendencies. All these symptoms have occurred in patients who never previously experienced a psychiatric disorder. This doesn't mean Steve will have these symptoms," she said. "But he could." She looked at me directly. "Are you willing and able to deal with this possibility?"

She had done an excellent job of freaking me out. But it mattered little because the Oregon Health Plan most likely would not pay for the therapy, which we could not afford.

"There are instances," she said, "where the drug manufacturer will provide the medication for free."

This was where things went sour between us, the diamond rock candy lady and me. I revealed my skeptical and defiant nature, for I viewed any benevolence on the part of a drug company as suspect and believed that as a corporation their highest priority was profit. I didn't know that a decade in the future one particular drug company's research would carve out a new future for Steve, a future that in this moment with the diamond rock candy lady seemed bleak.

"Why would they do that?" I asked. "I've never heard of a drug company wanting to help people for free. There's got to be a catch, some ulterior motive."

I'd blown it. She peeled back and dropped her previously sympathetic demonstrations like a practitioner's used latex glove into the garbage. Offended by my conspiracy theory, she defended the drug company as a stockholder would and then turned away and diverted all her attention toward Steve for the remainder of the visit, not saying another word to me. She did, however, write me an order to have my blood drawn and tested.

❂

Craig's wife called and asked if I would come sit with her and the body. When I arrived, Craig lay in his bed, waxen and gray, eyeballs no longer fluttering behind closed lids, arms crossed over his chest below the white sheet. Craig's wife had notified the mortuary but requested they not remove his body for forty-eight hours so the local Buddhists could pray over it. I sat in one of the two chairs next to the bed, his wife in the other. Craig's skin looked ashen and translucent as a blown-out candle. I wanted to touch it, feel for myself if the texture betrayed the appearance, but I didn't touch the thin layers of skin tissue, the fabric containing the HIV virus. It's one thing to look at a dead body; it's another to feel it.

After a time, we moved to the kitchen table. She told me they were engaged to be married when he tested positive for HIV ten years earlier. She had her dress picked and ready. But the discovery shocked them into canceling the wedding. She passed me Craig's old photo album. Among the photos I saw a young, hippie Craig—here, with a group of long-haired friends standing beside a colorful school bus, and there, holding hands with a bare-breasted woman as they stood facing one another. There was also a series of photos of Craig embracing a man from behind, his arms flat on the man's chest, an ease and intimacy reflected in this touch that, in life, I never saw Craig exhibit. "That's Joe," she said. "He's been meditating in a cave ever since I notified him that Craig was nearing the end. I've often wondered if they were lovers." I stared intently at the photos, at Craig's uninhibited tender embrace, the way the friend held him back, the sheer joy in both their smiles.

Later, his wife told me she had written a letter to Craig's previous girlfriend, the innocent twenty-one-year-old from seven years prior, to say she should get an HIV test. Craig hadn't informed her of his status, and throughout the course of their affair they had unprotected sex. She went on to tell me that a circle of people in Colorado, where Craig worked selling his wares every summer, was now divided by Craig's lack of disclosure. Some had been exposed, while others had not. The news created quite a convoluted mess amidst partners and friends as she contacted every person she suspected might be at risk.

How she knew all this, I didn't know. I assumed Craig confided in her. Perhaps she was the only one he was truly honest with. For he certainly kept secrets from us—like the fact that he was HIV-positive and knowingly exposed others to HIV without informing them. This fact was none of my business, but once I became privy to the knowledge, it profoundly complicated my memory of Craig.

When she first arrived, this woman who became Craig's wife, this woman we had never heard word of, Steve and I often wondered where she came from. Why is she here? Why now? They seemed such an unlikely couple, with her twenty years his senior. She appeared more like a mother figure or a trusted friend. Then it dawned on me, as she relayed this story, that perhaps she was the only one all these years to have known Craig's HIV status. Perhaps because of his determination to keep his status secret, she was the only one who could care for him.

The first time I saw Craig, I was six months pregnant with Lily and had gone to see a house for rent that was advertised in the paper. I climbed the steps to the front porch and had barely peeked through the window when I heard from behind me, "Can I help you?" in a thick New York accent that sounded nasally to my west coast ears. I turned to find a man of slight build and height with long raven hair and alabaster skin wrapping a chiseled jaw, eyes so intensely blue it was as if I were looking into the depths of Crater Lake. The prospect of a baby being born on his property excited Craig, and he was eager to rent to us. We lived there for eighteen months until Craig helped us buy our own property with a loan toward the down payment.

It wasn't until Craig's death, when I learned of his ill choices perpetrated on a group of people I never knew, that I questioned his character. The Craig I knew was a nice man—an odd man, certainly, an eccentric man, absolutely—but was he a man lacking care and compassion for others? I couldn't imagine anyone in his or her right mind consenting to unprotected sex with an infected person. Especially in 1996, when an HIV-positive diagnosis was largely considered a death sentence. Craig exposed others. Knowingly. This idea rattles me to my core: that someone—anyone, but certainly someone I considered a close friend—could be capable of this type of malicious intent. What kind of person does such a thing? A person with bad blood? A bad heart? Was his heart poisoned by all the microbes pulsing through his valves, gushing, swishing, whooshing from chamber to chamber, traveling the sixty thousand miles of veins and arteries of his body?

IV.
According to the CDC, "The overall risk of an infected [pregnant] mother transmitting HCV to her infant is approximately 4 – 8 percent per pregnancy. Transmission occurs during pregnancy or childbirth, and no prophylaxis is available to protect the newborn from infection. The risk is

significantly higher if the mother has a high HCV viral load or is coinfected with HIV."

Sitting in a cushioned chair on a platform at the blood lab, the phlebotomist told me to hold my arm out, palm up on the arm of the chair. He tied an elasticized tourniquet around my upper arm, tapped on my forearm to get the vein to stand out, and inserted the needle.

"I hate needles," I said. I've had a fear of needles ever since being immunized as a child. It's not the sight of the blood that bothers me. It's the needle and the feeling of it pricking my skin, sliding into the vein, and then drawing out the blood. It makes me feel faint. It's the reason I have never given blood. A sorry excuse if ever there was one.

Staring around the room, I wondered if this young man knew what I was here for. Did it say on the lab request? Did he know to take special care, or was I just another arm to be pricked and therefore worthy of universal precautions? Do phlebotomists ever feel afraid? Do they approach each person as though he or she is a carrier of disease? Or are they jaded from their daily routine, careful in procedure, but not paranoid? Maybe he didn't need to be paranoid because I was paranoid enough for the both of us. *What if the result is positive? What if I've had hepatitis C all this time and didn't know it?* I thought. I could have passed it to my children. The thought agitated me so much I could almost feel viral microbes pulsing through my system.

He filled one, two, three vials, withdrew the needle, replaced it with a cotton ball, told me to hold it with a little pressure as he released the tourniquet and disposed of the needle. I stared at the three vials lying on the tray, mini plastic bottles of claret that surely tasted more metallic than like wine. What secrets awaited, hidden within those tubes? Good news? Or bad?

A week later I learned the results of the tests: negative. Relief washed over my body the way it does when I dive into a cool river on a hot summer's day. At least in regard to hepatitis C, I no longer had to worry about my children. That belief became obsolete seven years later when nineteen-year-old Lily walked into the house for a visit. I hugged her, and she winced. "Ow, my back, my back," she said.

"What's wrong with your back?"

"I got a tattoo."

"A tattoo! Are you serious? Let me see." She turned and lifted her hair, revealing a half-dollar-sized blue M with an arrowed tail curving to the right outlined in black just below her neck. "Why'd you choose that?"

"It's the symbol for Scorpio."

"Oh," I nodded. I wanted to say: What the hell were you thinking? Don't you know you could contract hepatitis C? But I refrained. She was playing the role of adult, and I had no jurisdiction over her anymore. I imagined her old and wrinkled one day, this symbol etched into her withered skin. I shook my head and said, "I don't get it. What made you decide to do that?"

"I had a dream about Sean that we got tattoos together. And since we're both Scorpios, I thought it was a good way to honor him."

There was no arguing with the spirit of a dead boy. Risk isn't dominated by physical intimacy. Sometimes it's the emotional risks that leave us fragile and broken: the risk of trust, the risk of abandonment, the risk of heart-break. I silently prayed that her blood flowed purely, that no virus microbes raced through her veins, multiplying. "You're not going to get any more, are you?"

A year later she came home with her own artwork inked into the top of her foot: a plumeria with three black tribal-looking lines extending like wings from each side of the flower. "It hurt so bad because of all the bones," she said.

"Well, good," I said. "Maybe that will cure you."

But it didn't. In another year's time she got a new tattoo. When I saw it for the first time, I finally broached the subject. "You know you can get hepatitis C from getting a tattoo, don't you?"

"Yeah, I know," she said.

"So, did you go to the same place as last time?"

"Yeah."

"Are they careful? Do they take precautions?"

"Yes, he uses new needles and ink and everything, and he opened it all up right there in front of me, fresh out of the package."

Well that's a relief, I thought as I stared at the painting on her lower leg: a dolphin diving below the ocean's surface, encircled by a quote, "Love the life you live. Live the life you love."

✪

Throughout the first night in the PICU after Akela's surgery, two nurses tend her and one other patient, darting back and forth between the two cubicles. Steve and I lie on the built-in window seat that acts as a bed, but sleep is impossible amidst the worry, the beeping monitors, and the rus-tling, murmuring nurses.

The next day, as I return to the cubicle from the restroom, a young student nurse intercepts me at the makeshift doorway, a gap between the wall and the accordion-style vinyl curtain.

"Hi," she says, a little too friendly and upbeat. "I'm involved in a research study on sepsis and am wondering if I could take a sample of your daughter's blood for the study." She smiles. "It would be used to help other children who suffer from sepsis."

I have no objection to helping other children. In fact, those words entice me. Yes, I think. I'd like to do what I can to help prevent other children from suffering as my daughter does, hooked to an IV drip of continual antibiotics and lactated ringers, morphine to manage the pain.

"Of course," says the student nurse, "I'd explain it to her and get her consent, so she'd know what is being asked of her. That way she can be a part of the process and know she is doing something to help other kids."

I think it strange she speaks this way. Akela is completely out of it; the most movement she makes is to wiggle her toes. There is no talking to her—at least there is no eliciting a response. She does not have the capacity to consent to taking part in a research study. *What is this woman thinking?*

"Let me talk to my husband," I say, luring Steve out of the cubicle to talk to the woman. She gives him her same cheerful pitch.

"By participating in the study, you'd be helping others," she emphasizes.

I feel conflicted. Those words she uses—"You'd be helping others"—are honest and true. But they also feel a bit manipulative. She wants our daughter's blood—our daughter's *infected* blood—because it is rare to have access to such a fresh contaminated specimen. And she wants it *now*, sooner than later, before the antibiotics have a chance to work their magic because, to her and her research, a healthy blood sample is worthless.

"I'd like to think about it," Steve says to the woman, who smiles another perky smile and says she will come back later. Once the woman is gone, Steve tells me he doesn't want any more of Akela's blood withdrawn. They have already taken multiple samples to run tests, and he thinks she's too weak to give more, that she needs every ounce of energy she has in order to heal. Part of me is disappointed to hear this. I am still stuck on those words—"Help others"—and I think if there is an opportunity to do so, we should participate. Another part of me feels bombarded by the woman's request. Maybe it is her demeanor. Maybe it is simply being put on the spot to give at a time when I have little energy for it. We are in the PICU not because we want to be, but because we have to be.

When she returns, Steve tells her he doesn't want to participate in the study. But I am not sure we have made the right decision. There seems to be a dichotomy we are not living up to—the yin to the yang, or vice versa. The doctors gave Akela blood products during surgery in order to help her heal. Those blood products were, hopefully, pure and clean and would aid in her healing process. The donation was a gift. And now we have the opportunity to make a donation of our own: a sample of Akela's sepsis-infected blood, a rare commodity, for the sake of science, a potential gift of knowledge to future sepsis-sufferers. Our decision prevents us from completing the circle of recipient-donor exchange. And for years, I will question this decision.

✪

Shortly after Craig's death, in my weekly writing class, I offered to read what I had written:

> He totters out the back door toward me to where I wait on the open deck by the garden bench. He is wearing pajamas, a robe, slippers. As he teeters from side to side, his wife follows behind, arms outstretched, ready to catch him should he fall, like a mother following a baby learning to walk. I wait patiently, although it is unnerving to see him this way, a once vital man now barely able to walk. At this time, I have no idea what is wrong with him.
>
> "Hi Laurie," he says.
>
> It is the last time I ever hear him speak my name.

My teacher approached and stood looking over my shoulder at me and my paper. "What did he die from?" she asked.

I faltered. I had told no one in our valley. Craig's condition was a secret burrowed into my soul the way bacterial and viral microbes penetrate cells. Both Craig and his wife's steadfast desire to hide his condition pressured me, in a direct request, to remain silent. So I had. I internalized their secret. And as I watched Craig's decline, without anyone to talk to, save for Steve, the knowledge of the truth whittled away at my insides. My own private dis-ease. *Do I dare reveal it? What if somebody suspects who it is?* I stared down at my lap, ashamed. But was it my shame I felt or his? Is it possible to feel another's shame or only imagine it? Maybe it was a combination of the two: my projection of what he must have felt mixed with my own inner conflict for aiding and abetting his retreat into hiding. Or maybe the shame I felt was the net society had cast over those who suffer the disease, whether infected physically or emotionally.

I summoned my courage, and for the first time I said, "He died from AIDS."

V.

Ten years after Steve's diagnosis, his general physician suggested he return to gastroenterology to enquire about treatment. He had not been back since he was seen by the diamond rock candy lady. At his appointment, they told him their office would be participating in an upcoming trial for a new combination therapy that did not include interferon, the medication with all the extreme side effects. Previous trials of this new therapy had displayed a ninety-percent success rate, and the new nurse practitioner believed Steve was the perfect candidate based on his age and wellness. As a guinea pig in a drug trial, all his medication and healthcare would be free. The news dizzied us from our mutual-held breath. Did we dare believe he would be accepted into the study? And beyond that, did we dare believe he had a real shot at being cured?

The nurse practitioner advocated for Steve, and the drug company gave him a provisional "yes." The trial would start in a couple of months. Everything looked good. It seemed like a sure thing. But before the trial began Steve had to have an ultrasound on his liver and blood drawn for tests. The results of the ultrasound were good, but one of the blood tests showed he had a low platelet count.

They dropped him from the study.

This news made me fold in on myself. This vast future that had been laid out before us in the form of possibility had been eradicated as quickly as it had been presented. But the bad news didn't place Steve in a worse predicament than he already was in. Before being accepted into the study, he had chronic HCV. After he was dropped from the study, he still had chronic HCV. But that shard of hope revoked, the disappointment, it was like a hole within emptiness.

When the gastroenterologist reviewed the results of Steve's platelet count, he discovered the low count did not signify something inherently wrong with Steve, but rather that he had abnormally large platelets; therefore, there were fewer of them. Steve went to the hospital for a liver biopsy, which determined that in the ten years since his last procedure, his liver had gone from a stage II to a stage I—a reversal virtually unheard of, yet one that could be attributed to lifestyle changes: regular meditation practice, taking milk thistle seed, and quitting alcohol—all positive influences on Steve's health. Still, the nurse practitioner informed him that this improvement could have been the result of an inaccurate biopsy. Stage I or stage II, it didn't matter. Either stage qualified for participation in the trial. The gastroenterologist and nurse practitioner, a married couple, advocated for Steve to be readmitted into the study, but he was once again rejected based on his low platelet count. The nurse practitioner persisted. She bypassed the person determining who may or may not participate in the trial and appealed to the person at the top rung of the study. She wrote a letter from her husband's e-mail detailing the reason for Steve's low platelet count, his phenomenal health considering he'd had HCV for forty-five years, and the condition of his liver. She then signed her doctor husband's name.

And just like that, Steve was accepted back into the study.

On the morning of the first day of the trial, Steve was required to fast so they could get a clear reading on his viral count when they drew his blood before his first dose of medication. "I'm going to be the first person to be viral free within a week," he said to the nurse practitioner. She drew his blood. The viral count: 500,000 parts per milliliter. He took his first dose. Two hours later, she drew his blood again. The new viral count: 10,000. Two hours after that she drew it again. The viral count: 81. And as if all he had to do was state the affirmation, after one week on the medication his viral count was undetectable. But they didn't label him virus free. Viral microbes could have been hiding somewhere in the blood. The following week, it was a party in the examination room; all the doctors and nurses in gastroenterology wanted to see and celebrate the guy who had been declared virus-free after two weeks on the medication. But even though he had been declared virus-free, he was required to continue the prescribed twelve weeks of medication, and they would monitor him for the following year to make certain the virus would not return.

Everywhere he went Steve carried with him an insulated, zippered cold case full of pastel color-coded pill bottles resembling dyed Easter eggs in green, yellow, blue, and pink, labeled ABT 333, ABT 450, ABT 267 and Ritonavir. Every Tuesday for twelve weeks, he woke and made a cup of bitter green tea, for he was not allowed to add his usual honey and milk on test days until after they had done the blood draw, and I made him a scrambled egg sandwich with cheese and avocado for him to eat afterward.

"I'm supposed to eat lots of fat to assimilate the medication to the best ability," he said. So for three months we were on a high-fat diet of fettuccine alfredo, quiche, scalloped potatoes, spinach and three-cheese lasagna, and avocados, avocados, avocados. I didn't need the extra fat, but extra pounds on my body were a welcome condition for the prospect of Steve having more years within his.

After six months, Steve was proclaimed "cured."

❂

I often wonder about Craig's intentions. Did he merely desire to be close to others? Was he craving touch, the warmth of another body so as not to feel isolated? Was sex for him a substitute for emotional intimacy? Did he fear being denied such intimacy if he were to be honest with his partners, or was he just pissed off that he had contracted a deadly disease and took it out on whomever he could? These are questions I'll never have answers to. I ask them because facing that fear of contagion that gave me pause in signing the consent form in the PICU lies somewhere in understanding Craig's actions. They are directly linked: bad blood, contagion, risk, intent—malevolent or not.

When Akela needs blood products in 2007 to stabilize her healing, it is no longer considered a death sentence for those diagnosed with HIV. But when Craig died in 1996, that outcome was just beginning to change for the better; he died on the pivotal cusp of advances in treatment. My emotional body, tainted by a fear of contaminated blood that has dwelled since Craig's death, seems to have frozen in time. Akela doesn't contract a blood-transmissible disease from the donated platelets. And her condition improves to a full recovery. Still, during part of the three weeks she spends in the hospital, her blood is infected. It seems bad blood manifests in more ways than one.

❂

At home, I pull the down comforter back to strip the sheets for washing. On Steve's side there is a dark burgundy spot from where he scratched at a scab. I peel off the sheet to discover that the spot has soaked through to the mattress cover. In the past, every time Steve would nick one of his fingers, get a scratch or cut, I imagined microscopic organisms swarming through the droplets of blood, infecting his cells, reproducing, mutating, and even though I'd try to fight it, I'd feel my limbs retreat, keep my distance. But now I experience none of this. I pause, considering whether or not to wash the bulky mattress cover along with the sheets. I stare at the stain. For the first time in a decade, I feel no fear when confronted by Steve's blood. I decide to leave it.

REBOUND TENDERNESS

I nearly let my child die.

There it is—the stark truth, according to my mother's-guilt brain. It's been many years since it happened, but there was a time when this fact bored into my psyche the way carpenter bees bore into wood, settling there like an egg in a perfect hole inches below the surface. I avoided talking about it with anyone, even Steve.

This is how it would go if I could reverse time:

Akela comes home from the pizza parlor and says, "My stomach hurts." I quiz her like a professional, asking "Where does it hurt?" And even though she says, "all over," I ask more questions and run through a series of tests for appendicitis—despite the fact I have no medical training and only know now, in retrospect, what signs to look for.

I palpate the lower right quadrant of her abdomen, applying hand pressure slowly and gently with a quick release to check for sudden pain in that area. *Rebound tenderness.*

OR

"How does this feel?" I ask as I palpate the lower left side of her abdomen, pressing down slowly and gently then releasing quickly to check for sudden pain in the lower right quadrant. *The Rovsing's sign.*

OR

I have her lie supine and apply resistance to her knee as she flexes her right hip by raising her leg against the pressure of my hand. If she feels pain, I have her turn and lie on her left side and extend her right leg behind her to check again for increased pain with this movement. *The psoas sign.*

Once I finish these procedures, intuiting the signs of acute appendicitis, I whisk her to the emergency room, where the doctors confirm my suspicion and prep her for surgery to remove the unperforated appendix. They catch the appendicitis in the preliminary stages, and using laparoscopy, they slice into her with a one-inch cut that heals into a barely noticeable sliver of white near her bikini line. She spends at most two nights in the hospital and is back at the gym, working out with her gymnastics team, in a couple of weeks.

Yes, that's how it would go. Neat and clean and orderly.

This is how it actually went:

Akela came home from the pizza parlor two days after recovering from the flu and said, "my stomach hurts" to which I asked, "where does it hurt?" She said, "all over." I worried I had let her go out too soon after being sick and thought maybe she was having a relapse. I tucked her in and said good night.

She slept until noon and complained about her stomach when she awoke; then she began vomiting. Her temperature was 101 degrees. She had no desire for food, but I made miso broth and herbal tea and encouraged her to drink as much as she could as often as possible so she wouldn't become dehydrated. She spent two days in bed, getting up occasionally to go to the bathroom or lie on the couch in the living room. On that second day, she said she was feeling better and had relief from the previous stomach pain. But she was weak from the fever and vomiting and continued to rest in bed.

Later that afternoon, I walked into Akela's room to check on her while she was sleeping. Her face, normally alabaster in complexion, had a sallow pallor. I knew this look. I had seen it once before. It was the look of death. Five years earlier, my friend Terri, who had cancer, had this same sallow skin tone when she refused to go to the hospital to be treated for a common infection. We called the ambulance anyway. The doctors at the emergency room said that if we hadn't brought Terri in, the infection, not the cancer, would have killed her. As I looked at Akela's face, this memory flitted across my consciousness like a butterfly alighting on a flower, only to rise into the air and flutter away.

That was the moment. The omen I did not heed.

I checked on her, and on my way out, I closed the door behind me—unaware that her appendix had ruptured, giving her temporary relief from the pain. As she lay in her bed that afternoon, infectious organisms from the contents of her intestines seeped into her abdominal cavity.

But Akela survived. She survived a ruptured appendix, mild kidney and liver failure, sepsis, a compressed lung, two surgeries that left her with a five-inch vertical scar running the length of her abdomen, three weeks in the hospital, and months of recuperation.

In the immediate aftermath and during her recovery, friends tried to reassure me there was no way of knowing it wasn't the stomach flu that made my daughter ill, that a doctor might not have diagnosed it because she had atypical symptoms. I, too, tried to ease my self-blame by reading about the difficulty of diagnosis and talking to people who were either misdiagnosed or know someone who was, for there are quite a few. But it didn't help. Even though I could rationalize the circumstances that led to my not taking Akela to a doctor before her appendix burst, I could not rationalize the circumstances that followed. I was haunted by that butterfly memory, the one that flew away as quickly as it came when I checked on Akela that day. That was my greatest moment of carelessness. My worst in a lifetime full of mistakes. And even as I write these words, a part of me anticipates pointed fingers of judgment and blame—because those are the feelings I have wrestled with myself.

This is how I see it:

A mistake implies wrongness, a failing; something should have happened in a different manner other than it did. Mistakes inspire regret. And it seems the nature of regret is rooted in responsibility—whether the thing we regret is the result of our own mistake or that of another. Of course, some things are out of our control or "in the hands of God," as some people say and believe. Like terminal illnesses, which for the most part do not result from mistakes made by poor choices but, rather, assert themselves uninvited. But barring such circumstances or belief systems, then a natural response might be to trace a mistake back to its root. Rather than waiting for God to pass judgment, you might pass your own judgment and decide who or what is to blame for the wretched mistake that has now inspired your regret. It's a linked chain, this interconnectedness of mistake-regret-responsibility.

Here's the rub. If a mistake is not the will of God or fate or happenstance, then doesn't someone have to be held responsible? The link I have struggled with in my chain is Guilt with a capital G. I was responsible for my twelve-year-old child. I failed to get her to the hospital sooner than I did. The result: she nearly died. When I allow myself to think deeply on this, my chest tightens, restricts. For a long time, my punishment was to not let myself off the hook. For isn't it a mother's duty to not let her child suffer?

Even beyond duty, don't we have a biological instinct to protect our young, to ensure their survival?

For years, I craved absolution. If I were religious, I could have gone to confession and been cleared of my sin. But I'm not Catholic. I'm not Christian. I'm not anything—other than a woman who believes in kindness, the power of love, and in the unpredictability and beauty of nature. I am a woman who has failed, a mother who loves her child and got Lucky with a capital L.

There was a time when I wanted to write a letter to advice columnist Dear Sugar and have her—in all her compassionate star power and gentle, kind glory of advice giving—confront me on the role I played in this hard-luck pain of a story and then say to me, "It's not your fault, Sweet Pea; everybody makes mistakes," words that would have felt like the soothing caress of a hand stroking my head. But even as I desired such an empathic pardon, no such benediction would clear away the haunting. I realized that until the day I could accept that as a human in this life I am prone to making all kinds of shameful mistakes, until that day when this realization absorbed fully into the fibers of my muscles and the tissue in my lungs and I was truly able to allow myself forgiveness, a part of me would live as Guilt Mom, Neglectful Mom, Bad Mothering Mom. And so it was. I spent many a day identifying with these roles. I have often wondered—how many of us are there? How many of us carry a radical need to be washed clean of our flawed choices? Do not all of us in our longing for absolution from the acts of human frailty, whether we are religious or not, aspire to the divine?

During her appendicitis, before being taken to the hospital, Akela asked, not once but several times, "Am I going to die?"

"No, of course not," I said. I didn't know how close she was, or I didn't permit myself to know. To have this awareness meant acknowledging my daughter's mortality, greeting it at the door and welcoming it inside. In doing so I would have somehow been complicit, amenable to the possibility of losing my child. Denial can be powerful, inhibiting good judgment.

I still grapple with guilt over that one butterfly moment, although the intensity has faded. Louise Erdrich wrote, "Sorrow eats time. Be patient. Time eats sorrow." Maybe the same goes for the carrying of guilt. Or does that depend on the offense? I have a friend who said, when we were in our teens, that feeling guilty was pointless. She argued it only makes you feel bad without changing the previous outcome, which does no one any good, including yourself. I think she's right. It's the soul searching you do after you make a mistake that matters, the attempt to come to terms with the event, the resulting feelings, and then the ability to forgive yourself and achieve redemption. It's not easy. But guilt eats time the way sorrow does. So I will be patient. Time has allowed forgiveness to seep in and slowly eat the guilt.

Reprieve: Summer

The lawnmower blares. Steve pushes it in concentric swaths, starting at the outer edge of the lawn and moving inward. The exterior of mown lawn contrasts in relief with the shrinking interior of overgrown grass yet to be cut. Our border collie barks and lunges, snapping at the machine as it moves. Summer is not necessarily quiet here. Many days are filled with the sounds of upkeep and work. If it isn't the roar of our own lawnmower, it's the drone of the tractor at the nearby farm or the high-pitched whirring of a neighbor weed whacking. Steve mows weekly, but it grows so fast, sometimes he can't keep up. Shaved grass flies out of the mower. It leaves sporadic lines of wet clumps and a smell of fresh green, of swinging in a hammock, of lemonade afternoons on the verandah, even though we don't have a verandah. That fragrance of fresh cut grass that feels nostalgic? Scientists have determined it's actually a distress signal released by the grass.

The chickens roam freely. They scratch, one foot and then the other from front to back as though they are wiping their feet on a doormat—scratch-scratch with the left, scratch-scratch with the right. They dip their heads and with hard beaks peck at seeds and bugs—one, two, three—before scratch-scratching again. In the wake of this methodical behavior, they leave behind fertilizer droppings and a wreckage of disturbed mulch and exposed roots. They work their way up to the garden where the earthworms are fat and plentiful and the lettuce young and tender. We place scraps of chicken wire over the top of the lettuce bed in an attempt to prevent them from eating everything before we've gotten the chance. Steve gets annoyed. He does not want them roaming freely to demolish the garden. He yells and waves his arms, shooing them back down to the chicken yard, threatening to clip their wings.

The moist, fertile soil of the garden emits the sharp aroma of compost and manure. Amidst the eggplants, peppers, corn, and zucchini, cherry tomatoes grow tall and sprawling, their leaves a rich emerald, their developing fruit orange and red marble-sized orbs that glisten and entice. But when I reach for the tomatoes hidden in the middle of the plant, my arms become itchy, mottled with red that only cold water can relieve.

I hear a car drive up the gravel drive we share with the neighbor and turn toward his house. It parks near the pond, and the high-pitched chatter of small children echoes as they unload from the vehicle. In a matter of moments, happy shrieks ring out as they splash in the cool water. My children learned to swim in that pond, amidst the reeds and bullfrogs, fish and occasional snake, in water that went cloudy when the bottom got stirred as swimmers waded in and out along the edge, mud squishing between their toes. Back then, the neighborhood ponds were the summer gathering places where we all swam naked, uninhibited, catching relief from the dry midday heat. Kids would run and jump off the dock, tucked tight into cannonballs, a cascade of water rising in a great splash as they plunged. Babies would sit and crawl in the sand. Children just learning to swim dog-paddled and floated on their backs in life jackets. Mothers would talk as we kept our eyes on the children, constantly counting the number of bodies to make sure no one was lost beneath the surface. Nowadays, it is rare for the pond to have visitors. The most common sound comes at night when the bullfrogs sing. A raspy choir of ceaseless croaking in concert with the thrum and trill of crickets permeates the air.

I am in the kitchen when I hear a thump on the glassed-in porch, like something has fallen. I step through the sliding-glass door and see Lina, our long-haired calico cat, in the space between one of the windows and the open door that is folded back against it. She reverses with a tiny bird in her mouth. I can see the bird is still alive and will probably be fine if I can get it away from her. I have never seen Lina catch a bird. She is a poor hunter, much too slow. I know the only reason she caught this bird is because it had gotten stuck inside the porch and was easy prey.

"No, no, no," I say. "Let that bird go!" She trots out the open doorway with me following, still telling her "No!" I get a grip of her and open her mouth. A gray and brown house wren drops to the ground. I scoop it up before she can snatch it again. The bird gives a stunned shake and flies away toward the shade of the ash trees. I stand there for maybe thirty seconds, telling Lina, "You're not to catch little birds; they're our friends," when from the direction the bird has just flown, I hear the sound of a fall and landing. *Was it the bird falling out of the tree?* I turn to find the house wren in the clutch of our formidable hunter cat, Eóghain. This time the bird is askew in the cat's mouth, and I know it doesn't stand much of a chance.

I reach to grab Eóghain. She tries to slip away but is unsuccessful. I retrieve the injured bird and move to the shade. I want to lay it in the cool grass somewhere neither of the cats will find it, but Eóghain follows me, meowing, determined to reclaim her prize. I stand in the shade, whispering to the creature cupped in my hand, trying to soothe it. It's delicate, minuscule heart pattering against my palm.

I have held wild birds before. Both alive and dead. I have caught and saved hummingbirds, thwarting them from a similar wretched fate as the house wren currently in my hand. I've had birds sit calmly in my palm and then fly away in a whirl of buzzing wings. This time, this bird cocks its head this way and that, stretching its beak open. For a moment I think it is going to shake off the stun of having been captured a second time. But it is in the throes of death, the last gasps of air. Its heart stops. It goes limp in my hands.

THE POLARITY OF INCONGRUITIES

It's when near the beginning of your day, your husband, who has had chronic hepatitis C for forty-five years, comes home from the doctor's and says he has been declared "virus free" after two weeks in a drug trial for a new medication that awaits FDA approval. You jump up and down like a small child who has just watched a magician let fly a yellow chickadee from a previously empty hand. It's the exhilaration and disbelief of being blessed with such good fortune. It's knowing your husband's lease on life has been renewed, and therefore, so has yours.

Then, a couple hours later, your twenty-two-year-old daughter arrives home in tears. Earlier that morning at her boyfriend's house, she accidentally walked into the room where the body of his grandmother was being prepared for burial. She had died from lung cancer during the night. This is the first time your daughter has seen a dead body, and she now feels what it is to know that a person and a body are two very different things.

Several hours after that your younger daughter comes home from school and opens a large envelope to find a college acceptance letter offering her a $68,000 scholarship distributed over four years. She shivers with excitement and says, "It doesn't even matter if I get accepted to any other schools. Now I'm all set." It's feeling awed by her capabilities and thankful she is being offered a sound opportunity while also feeling relief that now you don't have to worry about the storm that might come if she is rejected by her top choice colleges.

It's washing dishes at the kitchen sink yet a few hours later in the early evening when all your family is out and finally allowing yourself to break in a great heaving gust over the unexpected death one week earlier of your friend Mary. You lean down, resting your forearms on the rim of the sink, and sob into the fading bubbles and dish gray water.

And all this happens on Valentine's Day. The day devoted to love, poetry, roses, and chocolate. A day rooted in the legend of a priest imprisoned for aiding the persecuted and performing secret weddings.

It's when a week later an official-looking letter arrives from a lawyer designating you as one of the beneficiaries of Mary's IRA and the rest of her small estate. You learn that you now have the means to send your daughter to college because even though she received a large scholarship, there will still be tuition to pay. It's suddenly having the ability to pay down the credit card debt and get your daughter the teeth implants she needs for the two upper lateral incisors she was born without due to genetic hypodontia, a congenital condition where some babies are born without some of their permanent teeth. It's the timing of things because oral implant surgery cannot occur until the age of eighteen when the jaw has finished growing, and your daughter is seventeen and a half.

It's when two months later you receive an acceptance to an artist residency in Vermont and discover you have been awarded a grant, of which you are overjoyed, but you realize there is still a hefty balance to be paid for the privilege of spending four weeks writing in a private studio overlooking a river, where they house and feed you and wash your dishes and linens. It's a fee you never could have considered paying when you applied for a full fellowship prior to the receipt of that official letter from the lawyer.

It's when four months after that you take your daughter 2,685 miles across the country to begin her freshman year of college in a place where neither of you knows a soul. It's the excitement, the giddiness, the nervousness, the apprehension—of saying goodbye. It's a feeling of satisfaction and completeness that as a parent you did something right by your child because she is not afraid of adventure and trying new things; she is whole and independent with a superb brain and fierce heart. And you can't help but feel thrilled because it's like unfolding a map to the future, so many places to go, so many possibilities. Only it's not a map to your future, but hers, and when it comes time to leave, all you want to do is grab her, pull her close, and hang on because you know this is that pivotal moment; once you let go, it will never be the same. Every day forward in her pursuit of autonomy, she will need you a little less. But you release her into her joy—because you have to.

It's arriving at the artist residency a month and a half later and meeting a new community of people from all over the world and discovering that it's possible to develop deep, meaningful relationships that bond you after just one week, and after two weeks you can't imagine ever going back to the life in which those people had no place. It's realizing that you made an unwilling trade: the loss of one dear friend, the woman whom you considered your godmother, in exchange for many new friends.

It's not walking a mile in another's moccasins—as the old saying goes—but walking in Mary's socks. For when you cleaned out her apartment in the days after her memorial, you took all of her Smart Wool socks even though they were much too big. As you wear these ill-fitting socks daily, you think about Mary: her tall and gentle grace made smooth by years of practicing yoga, how she never spoke an ill word of anyone even of those for whom others carried a mutual discontent, her effortless embodiment of acceptance and unconditional love. You think about how she never had children, how you, her best friend's daughter, are the closest thing to what she ever knew a daughter to be. And you contemplate how this wondrous experience you are having at this artist residency, in this place of maple syrup, apple cider, and autumn leaves, is made possible by Mary's death. This thought slices your heart to the quick because you don't know how you can ever go on without her, this dear friend who was a fixture in your life from the day you were born on the anniversary of her birth. And you know that she would be pleased to have made this possible for you, even though it meant dying. Because that's the kind of person she was.

The polarity of incongruities is evaluating life in this manner: between matters of the pocketbook and matters of the heart, between greeting new friends and saying that final goodbye, between loving and letting go. It's experiencing gratitude and grief—simultaneously.

THREE WEEKS:
A CHRONOLOGY FROM BEFORE TO AFTER

Before

First the house wrens returned. I watched tufts of insulation floating downward in front of the kitchen window. The birdhouse affixed to the exterior wall had not been cleaned since the previous year, and being wary of old nesting material, the wren pair began pulling insulation from a crack between the wall and roof. I don't think they intended to make their nest inside the crack. It was more their way of saying, "Hey, it's time to clean our house."

Steve pulled last year's remains from the tiny hole in the birdhouse, sprayed it out with a hose, and left it in the sun to dry. Back up it went on the wall, and the wrens promptly began their diligent and painstaking process of nest building, twig by twig, blade by blade of dry grass.

Then it was the robins' turn. Or maybe the robins came first. I don't know. They were discreet. All at once a fully-formed nest was wedged in the grape vines underneath the eaves of the house, visible through the vinyl windows of the bedroom loft, where Lily and Akela slept as young children. Aloof, the birds acted as if they were not present—or maybe more to the point, as if we did not exist. When we came upon them either perched in the pine tree or pecking in the grass, they flew away, attempting to fake us out. Sometimes I watched them fly from tree to tree, always up high, before cautiously approaching the nest, but only when all threat of our movement was gone. Once the babies arrived, though, they became more tolerant, as the demand to constantly fly to and from the nest was of the highest priority.

The wrens were quite communicative. They sang sweet little songs as they went in and out, stopping to perch in the coral honeysuckle that vines its way against the wall opposite the nest. They seemed not only to talk to one another in their steadfast work but reveled in the action of nest building. Like the Seven Dwarves, they whistled while they worked. Sometimes, their song turned to sqwawks as we passed on our way to the laundry room or outhouse. They made the most ruckus when we turned on the water to take a shower, for the old claw-foot tub lives underneath the birdhouse. Often, I found twigs in the bathtub, dropped remnants that did not fit through the birdhouse's small openings. I'd try to toss them someplace strategic where they could retrieve them and try again, but they never did, preferring instead to find new nesting material.

May 23

Two days before Memorial Day, my neighbor's dog was attacked by a cougar in the bright late afternoon light. This neighbor had been lounging on his deck, relaxing and enjoying a drink, when he heard screams that his land-mate described as sounding like someone was being murdered. He ran toward the sound, through the woods behind his house, until he saw his black dog upside down with her legs in the air. He couldn't understand what was wrong with her. The cougar blended into the environment so well it was perfectly camouflaged until he nearly ran right into the animal. He abruptly stopped just feet from where the cougar lay on the ground with the dog's head in its mouth. They locked eyes, my neighbor and the cougar. The man then stomped his foot multiple times and yelled. The cougar released the dog and, in two great leaping bounds, disappeared into the forest.

The dog suffered multiple puncture wounds to the face, head, and neck, which swelled and required antibiotics, but aside from the minor wounds and the severe trauma of finding itself within the jaws of a very large cat, the dog was fine. The rest of us, however, were put on alert, keeping watchful eyes on beloved pets. I brought our dog, Roxy, who was used to sleeping outside (and in fact preferred it), into the house each night. A few more sightings occurred in the days that followed—once on the deck of a couple's home and again at the convergence of their driveway with the road.

Occasionally, I find cougar scat on the ridge trail and, a few times, in our yard. Twice, one of my neighbors has come upon a cougar in a tree along the ditch road as he was walking his dog early in the morning. Just the year before, around 8:30 p.m., we heard the eerie, primal sound of a pair mating in the woods only a couple hundred feet from our house. But an attack on a domestic animal close to someone's yard, however well hidden by the forest, and in bright daylight hours is the exception. Such wild boldness elicits small pangs of paranoia. But that's life in the borderlands of the wilderness.

May 27

I saw it from a short distance, but I couldn't tell what it was. Not long before, one of our hens had flown to the top of the chicken run gate and then hopped onto the roof of the hen house. I told her to go back, but I didn't move to do anything about her escape. I knew she wanted to scavenge for fresh bugs and greens. And why not? If I were a chicken, even if I had ample space to roam, I'd want to escape too. So I let her be, not worrying about predators and figuring that when it came time, I'd open the door and let the hen back into its generous confines. Later, when I glanced in that direction, seeking signs of the hen's roaming, I puzzled over something bird-like that looked to be hanging in the shade of the ash tree right behind the chicken house. Was it the chicken? Had she gotten caught in the tree when she flew down from the roof of the coop? *Nah, she would have made a racket if she had gotten stuck*, I thought.

Whatever it was, the thing wasn't moving, but floating, suspended in the air the way stuffed birds are displayed in natural history museums. I could see soft, downy fluff, emphasized by the sideways forest light that glanced through the trees, and what looked like wings spread in a wide fan.

As I moved closer, I saw it was a dead owl, hanging upside down by one elegant, stretched leg. It appeared to be caught in a dead and dried blackberry cane that, when the tenacious weed had been green and alive, had climbed into the branch of the ash tree. The owl's talon was curled as if gripping the blackberry cane, but on closer inspection, I found that the cane was not in the owl's grasp at all, but rather, the owl was in the grasp of the blackberry cane, barbed as it was to its soft feathers, which resembled the tan plush fur of a rabbit. The owl was hooked from creamy-tan talon to coffee-brown breast, its wings splayed wide open, feather by delicate feather, silently grasping air that no longer supported flight. The wings were a muted milk-chocolate brown flanked by white spots that reached from shoulder to tips in gradient rows. Its short tail matched its wings: it, too, spread at the ready. The other leg was bent, its talon a closed but empty fist. And underneath, at the bottom, hung a round, dark head, loose and pliant at the end of its fourteen-vertebraed neck, with a white brim over its closed eyes and the bridge of its curved beak.

Some believe owls are omens of death, an attribution that has clung to these soundless night fliers since ancient Roman times. Once, many years ago, when I was driving home late at night along a quiet country road, I hit an owl. Or it hit me. Out of the blackness, it thunked hard against my windshield. I stopped and retrieved it, laying the dead bird with the broken neck on the passenger seat. The next day I got a call that my aunt had died of a heart attack while in bed the night before.

A couple months before finding the floating owl behind the chicken coop, my pregnant daughter, Lily, was driving home late at night when a large barn owl flew straight at her windshield in a feathered mass of brown and white, talons directed toward the glass as if reaching out to grab her. She hit the brakes, and the talons grazed the window. Upon hearing this, I could not help but fear the owl was a portent of some unwelcome doom. Normally in life, I do not allow superstition to dictate my actions, yet there have been times, such as this, when my core was jostled by the mysterious implications of contact with a wild animal. I am not a prayerful woman. My beliefs lean more toward the magic of nature than God. Still, when my daughter told me of her brush with the owl, I said a prayer for the safety of her and her unborn child.

I don't believe owls are an indication merely of bad luck. Once, on a September evening when we lived in town, Steve and I sat at the dining table adjoined to the open-air kitchen, midstream in a heated argument. This was during what I now affectionately refer to as our "successful marriage counseling days." I don't recall what the fight was about or how it began. I do, however, distinctly remember how it ended. A miniature owl swooped in through the open back door, landing upside down and clinging by its talons to the edge of the window seat that was covered in potted house plants. At first, we thought it was a bat. But we discovered it was a yellow-eyed owl that could fit into the palms of our hands. That was the end of our argument. In one swift swoop, the energy shifted from animosity to curiosity and wonder.

On the day I found the owl affixed to the blackberry cane, two days after Memorial Day and the same day that Akela was due to arrive home from a year studying abroad at a French university, the significance of finding a dead, floating owl, caught and preserved upside down in mid-flight, certainly left me wondering about such things as omens and prophecy. That morning, I had received a message from Akela in Europe: forty-five minutes before she arrived at the Brussels airport, a massive power surge knocked out all air traffic control and backup generators. Belgium's air traffic control is linked to the mothership at Brussels airport. This power surge wreaked havoc on the entire country: no flights in or out within its borders. Like the suspended dead owl, all possibility of flight had been rendered nonexistent.

Gently, I released the blackberry barbs from the owl's feathers and cradled the bird in my hands. I was tempted to dismantle the wings from its body and keep them—so beautiful they were, fans perfectly rendered in matching formation. Instead, I folded them into a resting position. Pungent spearmint wafted into the air as I stepped through the patch to where I had dug a hole. I bent down and placed the owl in the damp soil, took one long look, and covered it up.

May 28–29

In France, Akela had found her first love. Sounds romantic, doesn't it, finding love in France? It is. Until it ends and it's time to say goodbye because she lives in Oregon and he lives in Slovakia, more than five thousand miles away.

When her flight was cancelled, the airline had put Akela up in a hotel for the night. She loaded her four bags, which her boyfriend helped bring on the train from France, onto a shuttle, and then she watched through the window as her first love grew smaller and smaller until he disappeared. Mere days before, they had locked their love onto the Pont des Arts Bridge—one of two bridges known as "love locks" bridges in Paris that cross the River Seine, where couples fasten padlocks inscribed with their initials to symbolize their love and then throw the key into the river.

On this day, though, the Brussels airport reopened, and Akela boarded her flight. She sat in a window seat on the plane, watching the life she had led for nearly a year disappear from her view. She sobbed, inconsolable, as the woman in the aisle seat tried to comfort her across the divide of an empty middle seat.

The third and final leg of her flight home was cancelled due to mechanical problems. She was rebooked onto a flight to Eugene, and Steve drove three hours to pick her up. She arrived in the middle of the night on my forty-ninth birthday. I got up out of bed to greet her, relieved she had made it home safely.

During

I began to wake in the mornings to rustling in the grape leaves. That's how I knew the baby robins had arrived. It wasn't because the babies started peeping. Unlike newborn humans, baby birds do not come out of the egg with the capacity to scream. It takes time for them to grow strong enough to raise their beaks to the sky, mouths agape in search of nourishment. The chorus of peeps grew slowly, from soft murmuring like tapping drumsticks to a crescendo of crashing cymbals. Each parent bird a conductor, the worm or caterpillar in its beak the baton that waved to increase the volume until the cries hushed with the flapping of wings as the parent flew off in search of the next mouthful.

May 30

Akela's tears wouldn't stop. "I didn't want to come home," she said. "I almost didn't get on the plane. I shouldn't have. I should have stayed. It hurts so much, Mom. Why won't it stop? Make it stop!" she cried.

I don't know how it is for others, but for me, the worst part about being a parent is watching my child experience pain, whether it is physical or emotional. I had already witnessed Akela suffer intense physical pain in her life. Now, I was witness to the kind of pain no surgeon or hospital could cure: heartbreak. She cried for me to erase the pain, but there is no solace for the loss of first love other than time. I tried to be wise and supportive. The best I could do was coo like a dove in words that, while true, also felt futile and overwrought.

"You never know what life will bring you. It's a mystery," I said.

In private, my tears flowed almost as freely as my daughter's. My body felt consumed, pulsing with heartache on a cellular level as though the breakup was happening to me. I couldn't shake it. Empathy had barbed me the way the blackberry cane had caught the owl. It was as if I were that owl just before death—upside down, wings splayed, flailing hard to break free, being crushed under the weight of gravity, tethered and exposed.

May 31

At seven-thirty in the morning, I lay in bed still adrift in sleep when the chickens began squawking uproariously. Something about these squawks was different from their usual gad-about-the-chicken-yard calls in the morning. An electric door opener set on a timer lets the hens out early and closes them in at night once they've returned to the coop to roost. The only times we've had problems with predators is either when the door hasn't closed due to an electrical error and a fox or raccoon has invaded the coop or when the door has shut before all the hens have made it safely back inside for the night. On this morning, the chickens were roaming their yard, making a racket. But one hen's screeches stood out above the rest, so I went outside to investigate.

As I approached the gate to the chicken run, I could see through the window into the coop that the chickens were hiding inside. I opened the door and counted. Six hens. One was missing. "Here, chickie, chickie," I called. From the very back of the run, out of the thicket of ash trees, came our white hen. She did her best to run toward me, but she was limping. Loosened feathers fell from her underside. She entered the coop, and I closed the door.

"Get out of here!" I yelled at the predator toward the back of the chicken run. "Scram! Shoo! Go away!"

Later, I entered the chicken run. In the center of the open area, pure white feathers lay in a scattered heap where the fox had caught the chicken. I followed the path of feathers that led through the brush. Underneath a bush, there was evidence of where either the fox paused to hide with its stolen treasure or where the hen took refuge after being released from the predator's grasp. Farther still, feathers led in a line, where they stopped abruptly at the fence, woven as it is through the evergreens. Gray foxes climb trees. And fences too. Evidently not so well, though, when they have a live chicken in their mouth, and it doesn't help when a perturbed woman starts screaming at them.

June 3

The text arrived while I was swimming laps at the YMCA. Two sentences: "How are the transcriptions coming? It's time to wrap that up."

The transcriptions were from audio recordings I had made of my friend, Christy, who was living with inflammatory breast cancer in Denver, Colorado. I say "living with" because despite the extreme pain and suffering she endured—and she endured more than I thought humanly possible—Christy did not like the usual terminology of "fighting a battle" attributed to patients with cancer. She thought it implied that if she lost the battle, she hadn't tried hard enough and her death could be construed as a failure on her part. Christy did not think of herself as a warrior; she professed to avoid conflict.

Still, she did acknowledge that cancer was her foe and she (and every one of her breast cancer sisters) were fighting for their lives. Because in her words, "What else can you do but fight?" Inflammatory breast cancer is rare, deeply aggressive, and commonly not diagnosed until it presents as stage IV cancer with little chance of a cure. Statistically, it is a losing battle. Christy actively participated in every remotely possible strategic plan offered to extend her life. That's what concerned her most. Staying alive. Christy just wanted to *live*—hard and well, like she had done every day—hiking, traveling, running marathons, teaching writing, finishing her memoir, spending time with friends and family—even before she knew her life would be shorter than most.

When I received her text, I knew those words, "it's time to wrap that up," signaled the end was not only near, but imminent. She would not have sent me the text if her situation were otherwise. *It's time to wrap that up.* That's what someone says when they are certain of not the number of finite days, but the reality that there *is* a number and the number is shrinking rapidly.

The transcriptions were for a book of "Crazy Aunt Christy" stories she wanted to leave for her two adolescent nieces, something they could refer to throughout their lives and always remember her by. I had pushed finishing them to the edge of what was reasonable or appropriate. Was this because I was in denial of Christy's circumstances? Or was it because life was happening at what seemed like an accelerated rate all around me—my younger daughter devastated by the separation from her first love, my older daughter due to give birth to her first child in two and a half weeks. Newness and change. Tenderness and worry. Birth and death. Transformation. I was searching for the strength to continue being a supportive mother to both my daughters, to say nothing of the potential loss and impending doom I felt as a friend.

The baby shower was in two days. The blessingway two days after that. I determined that I would devote the day after the blessingway to transcriptions.

That same day in Paris, a week after my daughter and her boyfriend had locked their love onto the Pont des Arts Bridge, Parisian authorities began the removal of nearly one million padlocks deemed a structural hazard to the safety of the "Love Locks" bridges. Sixty-five tons of everlasting love. All those pledges, all those wishes, affixed to the metal grates, were ripped away by a crane and disposed of.

But down below, at the bottom of the Seine, still lie the keys to all those hearts.

June 7

We gathered to celebrate the approaching birth of my first grandchild. It was one of those wretchedly hot summer days, and our circle of sixteen—squeezed between the mint patch, the shade garden full of lily of the valley, and the variegated elderberry shrub—formed an unintentional heart, for that was the shadiest and coolest part of the yard for an afternoon get together. First, we smudged with sage. Then after a few opening words by me—because as mother of the pregnant woman I was the host—one by one we went 'round the circle, singing songs, sharing stories, offering blessings on the mother- and father-to-be for a smooth labor and delivery. We imparted wisdom and encouragement on the new journey they were preparing to embark upon.

It's called a blessingway, a ritual rooted in Navajo ceremony that, since the seventies, has morphed into a midwifery custom. In these parts, it's a tradition that has supported birthing mothers for longer than my thirty-two years in southern Oregon.

We soaked Lily's feet in a warm bath laced with rose petals, lavender, and calendula while she got her hair braided with flowers—a change from one state of being to another—to symbolize her upcoming transformation from maiden to mother. Her feet were then massaged with cornmeal, and she was presented with a beaded necklace made during the ceremony—each person had added his or her own special beads, charms, or pendants to represent the wishes granted upon her, the birthing mother. A lapis lazuli bear for strength. A silver fairy for childlike imagination. A moon carved out of bone for the cycles. Amethyst for protection. Each bead a talisman—the sum of all its parts a birthing power-necklace woven from insight and caring.

As we went around the circle, our blessings were punctuated by the rise and fall of the robin babies' symphony, an echoing shrieking chatter. And on the opposite side of the house, the wren babies sang in a muted voice, yet no less palpable, no less insistent.

June 8–12

I finished the transcriptions the day after the blessingway and emailed them to Christy. She messaged me, saying "Send to [my sister] Melanie too.

In case I get incoherent. We're going into hospice care this week. Melanie may have to finish it on her own after I'm gone." Three days later, Christy entered a hospice care facility. The plan was for her to spend a couple days there to control the pain that had surged beyond Christy's high tolerance and then return home. But she never left the facility. She died the next night, at 11:15 p.m., forty-five minutes before her mother's birthday.

When I lost Christy, I was keenly aware that her loss was not my own. It belonged to her many friends, her sister and brother-in-law, her nieces, her father. But most especially, it belonged to her mother. Losing a friend is difficult. But losing a daughter—well, I'd like to say I can't imagine it, but I can because I almost lost one of my own. I know the only thing that eclipses watching your child suffer would be losing her, as Christy's mother had.

In the very near future, Lily would become a mother. She would join the ranks of women who bear witness to their children's pain—whether from scraped knees or the bite of a garden snake, a broken elbow or a ruptured appendix, maybe from bullying or the death of a friend to suicide, or, inevitably, from the heartbreak of a lost first love. This is why in the days that followed Akela's return from France, I cried as she cried. This is why in the days that followed Christy's death, I not only wept for the loss of my friend, but I wept for my daughter who was about to give birth. Because I knew she was entering a contract written with the beauty and color of flowers, as well as the bitter taste of hurt, disappointment, and loss. Yes, joy and love and celebration, too, but pain in measured doses.

After
In the week after Christy's death, as I awaited the birth of my grandchild (who would not make his arrival until two weeks after his due date), the yard and house grew silent. First the robins left. One morning I awoke to the empty space of a formidable lack of peeping. No rustling in the grape leaves. No squawking for food. The wrens left a few days later. I never saw them leave, didn't see the babies make their first flight from the nest into the coral honeysuckle, teetering uncontrollably as they alighted on thin branches, the way I saw the young robins do. The robin babies perched in the pine tree across the lawn from their nest. They were nearly the size of their parents. But there was a freshness to them, a hesitance. They flew from branch to branch, calling out to one another, seeming to cling to the familiar of their surroundings. But that lasted just the day. By the next, they were gone.

SOLVING MY WAY TO GRANDMA

1. "Mom, I have something to tell you. You might want to sit down."
   When my daughter said this, my first thought was *Uh-oh, who died?*
   Not *Oh my god, she's pregnant.*
   (Expect the _____)

2. The first words out of my mouth were: "You know, I've had an abortion." She did not in fact know this, because I had never spoken of it. I
   said it because I wanted Lily to know that abortion was an acceptable
   option. Afterwards, she told my secret to her sister, who implored
   me via text message: *When did you have an abortion?!* I conveniently
   avoided responding.
   (Two words: a term for when only part of a story is told)

3. When we had this conversation, Lily was a few weeks shy of turning
   twenty-five years old and one month into massage therapy school that
   Steve and I paid for by going into debt on our credit card while she
   lived with us and we supported her. Her boyfriend was twenty-one,
   jobless, without a driver's license, and lived with his mother.
      I got pregnant with Lily when I was twenty-two. I worked as
   a housekeeper at a bed and breakfast inn and delivered pizzas for
   Domino's. Steve worked as an auto mechanic. By the time Lily was
   born, I had turned twenty-three and Steve thirty-six. I had been on my
   own since I was sixteen. Together, we had little money, but we were
   independent.
   (A history of a character or person that tells what led up to the main
   story and promotes better understanding)

4. I suggested Lily have an abortion even though she was older than I was
   when I'd had her. "You can always have a baby later when it's the right
   time," I said. Yet when I became a mother, I didn't know what I was
   getting into and was wholly unprepared. Is there ever a right time for
   landmark decisions?
   (Behaving in a manner where one's words and actions are
   contradictory)

5. Akela got defensive in her sister's honor. "It's *her* decision," she said ac-
   cusingly. She thought my mentioning abortion was an attempt to sway

Lily's decision. She was right. But I realized being pro-choice does not mean the outcome will always be abortion. Pro-choice implies just what it says: a choice. And sometimes that choice is to have the baby. ("The first step toward change is awareness. The second step is _____." Nathaniel Branden)

6. I know we don't have control over much in life, not really. We can try our damnedest to control things, especially as parents. Sometimes we are successful and other times not. But a simple idea I had never considered before struck me deeply: as a parent, there is one thing we have absolutely no control over whatsoever: if or when we become a grandparent.
(A "lightning bolt" moment)

7. The mainstream, socially accepted, ideal American trajectory is you go to college, get a job, save money, get engaged, get married, save more money, build your nest, then have children. We did everything backward, Steve and I: we had a baby; bought land on credit; built a makeshift, illegal dwelling; had another baby; and then after eighteen years as a couple, got married and accrued student loan debt by going to college in our forties and fifties.
(Not conforming to type)

8. Throughout my daughter's pregnancy, I worried constantly. Would she finish massage school? If not, had we just gone into debt for nothing? Where would they live? How would they support themselves? Who would pay her car payment and insurance? Would her boyfriend get a job? Would the stress of having a child end their relationship? Would my daughter end up as a single mother? How much would I be called upon to help?
(High _____)

9. *I'm too young to be a grandmother*, I thought. I clung to the stereotype that grandmothers are old and white-haired and wrinkled. I wasn't done being hip and cool and rebellious. At forty-eight years old, I wasn't done being young. When I thought *Grandmother*, I thought Crone. Elder. Wise Woman. The last stage in the archetypal trinity of the Goddess, preceded by Maiden and Mother. One step closer to

death. These were not the terms in which I viewed myself, and certainly not the terms in which I wanted to be associated.
(Two words: Often happens in midlife)

10. Talk to nearly anyone and you will hear a story about a grandma who was a towering presence and influential force. I revered my own Grandma June: artist, painter, quilt maker, woodblock carver and printer. She baked chocolate chip cookies and stocked full the cookie jar on her kitchen counter whenever we'd visit. She read me *Eloise in Paris*, *The Jungle Book*, and *The Little Prince*. She taught me how to sew, crochet, and play piano. She took my brothers and me to Pescadero Beach where we built elaborate sandcastles, and she made gingerbread houses with us at Christmas. She traveled the world: China, Greece, Kenya, Turkey. You name it, she went there. Of all people, she was my favorite.
(Dearly _____)

11. In comparison to the ideal grandmother, I was off to a poor start—and the baby hadn't even been born yet! I often wondered how I would ever live up to my own expectations for the role. I dubbed myself The Worst Grandma Ever.
("The only thing we have to ____ is ____ itself." Franklin D. Roosevelt)

DOWN

12. Lily grew frustrated at my urging her to not have the baby. Everything in her body raged *Yes* to the future child, only the size of a pea. I knew this sensation. I had felt it on more than one occasion.
(My own heart's _____)

13. When I was nineteen, I had my first serious love affair. He was a thirty-one-year-old charismatic, obscure man, bordering on cuckoo, with a tendency toward anger and domination. From the beginning, he convinced me to get off the pill, citing how "unhealthy" it was. Like an impressionable fool, I acquiesced. Two pregnancies and subsequent abortions later, I learned there are worse things than taking birth control pills.
(Susceptible to physical or emotional attack or harm)

14. The first time I got pregnant, the decision to have an abortion was a no-brainer. The second time, though, my body wanted the baby and my spirit wanted it too. Still, my head said *No*. My boyfriend already had a toddler with a woman in another state. He never saw his child and did not accept responsibility for him. I knew I could not be bound to this man for life. I knew a child deserved better. I knew a superior father existed elsewhere.
(Opposite of simple, aka: It's _____)

15. Usually, the first thing people say when you tell them you are going to be a grandmother is *Congratulations!* Without hesitation. Despite the circumstances. It's an automatic response, like stopping at a red light and going at a green one. In our culture, it's expected that everyone is happy about becoming a grandparent.
(To assume is to make an ass out of u and me.)

16. My friend, Liz, who became a grandmother in her mid-forties, understood my turmoil. She had huge resistance to becoming "Grandma." But she said, with a knowing smile, "You're going to love it."
("_____is the daughter of experience." Leonardo da Vinci)

17. When Lily was six or seven months along, I bent down and said to her belly in a high-pitched, sing-song voice: "Hello baby, this is your Auntie Laurie."
(The path of least _____)

18. "What are you going to be called?" people asked. I thought hard about this. I searched the Internet for alternatives to the traditional "Grandma." *Savta* in Hebrew. *Mémé* in French. *Abuela* in Spanish. *Nonna* in Italian. *Yiayia* in Greek. *Oma* in German. *Amma* in Icelandic. *Bubbe* in Yiddish. *Bibi* in Swahili. *Babcia* in Polish. Nana, Gram, Grammy, Grandmother. I realized this would be the first and only time in my life I would choose my own name. The decision was overwhelming.
(In regards to 19-down)

19. I settled on "Bunny," a throwback to high school when I was called "Bun" because my last name is Easter, just like the holiday. This turned into "Grandma Bunny." Later, when Tristan will begin to speak, he will pronounce my name "Bubby." "Bubby! Bubby! Bubby!" he will sing in the sweetest, high-pitched voice, so full of love and wonder.
(Synonym for name)

20. Lily labored through the night, strong and resilient. I watched as a baby emerged from my own firstborn—the cord wrapped around his neck three times. He arrived unresponsive. The midwife put an Ambu bag over his face to stimulate breathing. "Talk to the baby," we instructed the new parents. It was two minutes before breath lit up his little body. But once he inhaled and his skin bloomed pink from oxygen, his eyelids opened in the most deliberate and graceful manner, like a ballerina's swooping *port de bras*, and he gazed about the room, fully present.
(To bear _____)

21. I held my grandson for the first time the day after he was born, swaddled in receiving blankets, dark eyes alert. He sucked hard on my index finger. People who are grandparents will say there is nothing else like it, that from the moment your grandchild is born, you feel instantaneous love.
("Beauty is _____, _____ beauty" John Keats)

22. When you become a grandparent, the dynamic shifts. You don't have any actual say in matters concerning your grandchild. You can express your views or offer advice (if and when it is requested), but your kid doesn't have to listen. She's the parent now, not you. She makes the decisions, and she decides how much of an influence you have with her child. In a certain way, you have to relinquish your identity as a parent.
(Sweet _____)

23. I don't know how it happened, but Tristan is the epitome of the Happy Baby, so good-natured and adaptable to his ever-changing environment. I often wonder if Lily realizes how lucky she is. Whenever he comes to visit, I play the *Ghostbusters* theme song and dance

ridiculously in front of him, singing "I ain't afraid of no ghosts!" He jumps up and down on his mother's lap, mouth wide open in a smile revealing his first two bottom front teeth, laughter erupting like the clattering of coins from a slot machine.

(When you win big, you hit the _____)

ANSWER KEY

Across: 1. unexpected 2. partial disclosure 3. backstory 4. hypocritical 5. acceptance 6. epiphany 7. atypical 8. anxiety 9. identity crisis 10. beloved 11. fear

Down: 12. desire 13. vulnerable 14. complicated 15. assumption 16. wisdom 17. resistance 18. indecisive 19. moniker 20. witness 21. truth 22. surrender 23. jackpot

Reprieve: Autumn

Pine needles are everywhere. They cover the grass, the fading flower beds, the roof, the paths, the driveway. They fall in gusts; each time a wind washes them from the two giant pines in the yard, down come the russet needles. They layer the ground in a slick and voluminous mulch. Sometimes, when I'm walking down the hill, the needles shift in a rolling fashion beneath my feet, which slide out from under me without warning. Down I go onto my ass, not nearly as graceful as the needles when they fly from the trees. Sometimes they poke my ass when I squat to pee, their ends sharp as surgical needle pricks. We rake and haul them in the wheelbarrow to dump onto a future burn pile. And then another explosion of wind brings down more. So we rake again. And again. This is all before the oak leaves fall, and the process of gathering continues.

The water for the hydro has gone out again. This happens usually when there is a storm and too much debris clogs the intake. But sometimes a bear will pull the pipe out of the water or bite it or even break it. Steve hikes to the source, more than two thousand feet away, up to the ridge and down the other side, through thickets of baby trees, over and under downed madrones and along the creek bed—the everchanging ecosystem that transforms with each season depending on the amount of wind and rain that passes through. This day, he strips off his clothes to wade waist-deep into the icy water, shovel in hand, to clear the debris from the pipe and dig out sediment that has washed downstream to fill the intake pool. This is solitary work in a place where only the birds and critters reside. It's a quiet place, other than the sound of the creek flowing or the wind whistling or an occasional tree rubbing against its neighbor. In the pool, the sound of the crystalline water cascading over branches and rocks is eclipsed by thundering footfalls coming down the hillside. A large black bear lumbers into the riparian zone just above where Steve works. He can see the undulation of its muscles beneath rippling thick fur as it moves. Quickly, he scrambles out of the pool, grabs his jeans, and tries to put them on. But he has no towel and hardly any time, and he struggles and staggers, standing on one foot on uneven ground as he tries to get the denim to slide over one wet leg and then the other, which if you've ever tried to dress in jeans when you're wet, you know is next to impossible. He nearly falls over. He's trying to be discreet, but he's making a ruckus in his getaway attempt. He flees, shoes and shirt in hand, and he can hear the bear following him through the forest at a distance. The next day, a generous pile of bear poop sits smack dab in the middle of the garden.

The leaves have barely begun to change color. They still cling to their branches, steady and resolute. There is no letting go yet happening here. There is love, though, and a little bit of faith. Maybe some grace. Although I confess, I've never fully understood what grace is in a spiritual sense. I was taught grace as a little girl, learning how to balance on one foot, practicing dance steps, the fluidity in *port de bras*, hands held in a certain fashion, thumb down toward the palm, pointer finger separate from the other digits, like an angel's hands, soft, delicate, graceful. If one moves with grace, does that make them any more god-like?

These days I move with purpose, up and down the hill multiple times a day, my arms strong, tossing firewood from the heap on the ground into the wheelbarrow then lifting the handles and balancing the heavy load on its single tire to push it around the pile of uncut logs waiting to be bucked up. We're stacking double rows balanced on wooden boards set on bricks to keep the wood from absorbing the moisture that will saturate the soil. The wood has been curing since the previous winter, a mix of oak and madrone from two trees near the house. One—the oak—had dropped a limb the size of a whole tree, threatening calamity. Once felled and cut into rounds, the interior of the trunk revealed itself to be severely rotten. The other— the madrone—had a cavernous hole at its base where the trunk met the ground, a tragedy waiting to happen. Now, they are split into fifteen-inch lengths suitable for the woodstove. The wood is dry in that seasoned way where when stacked, the split logs clang together, making a solid hollow sound that feels like peace, like warmth, a pleading knock of wood that echoes. I place each piece together in a jigsaw pattern, making sure the stack remains level and secure. Sometimes the pieces fit together naturally and with ease. Sometimes I need to flip a piece over, move it to another spot. Have you ever heard that expression "Let go, let God"? I think that saying implies that in order to have faith, one needs to surrender all capabilities. Perhaps, whoever came up with that slogan never split and stacked wood. They probably had a thermostat and just flipped a switch.

Of all the seasons, autumn is my favorite. What is it about autumn that evokes in me such an affinity? Is it the fact that both my daughters were born this season—one on a rainy day, the other in a swirling wind? Is it the measured changes that startle and awe? The cornucopia of crimson, gold, carnelian, and copper? Or is it the melancholy? A time of folding in on oneself, reflecting, preparing to enter the den like a bear for its winter sleep. Maybe it's the giving up, dying back, the fading of the light. The release and letting go. Leaves flying. Leaves falling. Leaves leaving. Is that why they are called leaves? For this ability to let go of their attachments, make ready to shed and leave their trees unclothed, bare, exposed. The thing is when a deciduous tree has lost its leaves, it makes way for more light, a more expansive view. You can see what normally is shaded. But not before a huge burst of beauty rings out—a surge—like a tree that is dying, how sometimes it gives forth a profusion of seeds, scattering the ground with them so that the following spring, after the hardship of cold, frozen earth and drenching rains, seedlings take root and emerge in a smattering of shoots. One tree becomes many.

ALL THE LEAVINGS

Only in the agony of parting do we look into the depths of love.
                                        —George Eliot

After visiting home for the week of spring break, Akela took leave of me at the airport—where so many leavings take place—to return to college on the opposite side of the country. She sat between me and Steve in the row of hard, black vinyl seats across from the security entrance, waiting until five minutes before her scheduled boarding. In the tiny airports of America's Podunk towns, where the lines are slim and the wait is short to nonexistent, this is the privilege of the rural folk—to leave passing through security until the last possible moment.

Before handing the TSA agent her boarding pass and ID, she hugged her dad and then hugged me, her arms squeezing tight around my middle, our faces pressed into one another's hair as we whispered our secret mantra into each other's ear. Our mantra has to do with love and longing and the ability of what we can hold—not in our hands, but in our hearts, sort of like clasping a wild baby animal, a rabbit or a bird, that instinctively attempts to squirm from your grasp, so the reflex is to clench tighter to keep it from escaping, knowing all the while that if you grasp too tight, you risk hurting the poor thing. That's what it feels like, this ability to hold. And we whisper this mantra to one another like a prayer at all the leavings.

This time, I didn't cry, which feels foreign to me.

❈

When I was in first or second grade, at the end of each day the class haphazardly filed into two lines to leave the classroom, singing: "*Adios, amigos.* Goodbye, friends. *Hasta la vista.* Until we meet again."

☉

My Bohemian great-grandmother, Anna Juza, would have said, *Sbohem*, as she waved goodbye to her homeland while emigrating from what is now the Czech Republic. The first of my Irish ancestors to arrive in North America in the 1600s would have said, *Slán*, as he left the shores of the Emerald Isle. My German ancestors would have said, *Auf Wiedersehen*. When Akela leaves France to return to the States after a year studying abroad, what will she say?

Au revoir, Goodbye? *Adieu*, Farewell? À *bientôt*, See you soon?

☉

Leavings are described in all manners of words, depending on the circumstances. One might depart from a ship or embark on a journey. Quit a crappy job or retire from service. Clear out, go forth, push off, or say goodbye. Sometimes, one needs to escape a bad marriage, prison, or reality. Break away from the mold. Abandon, desert, forsake. One might simply move to a new residence while others must flee for safety. Defect for artistic, religious, or political freedom. Sometimes one is forced to vacate the premises or told to beat it, scram, vamoose. Children are often expected to run along; then, as adolescents, they learn how to give the slip, and later, in defiance, tell adults to take a hike. Sometimes it is best to let one alone to solve her own problems. Sometimes, though, when problems seem insurmountable, she may withdraw into herself, which presents a bigger challenge than, say, withdrawing money from the ATM before disappearing from town or withdrawing before climax because no condom was handy. Sometimes there is an urge to ride off into the sunset. Always, if there is a fire, one needs to exit the building.

☉

The first concert I ever attended was when I was ten and went to see John Denver at the Cow Palace with my mom and two older brothers. I snuck a cassette recorder in my mother's purse, the size of which consumed the entirety of her leather handbag, and I recorded a bootleg tape. The quality was poor. But I listened to it on repeat, flipping from side A to side B and back again while I hit tennis balls against the garage door.

John Denver's songs were a staple growing up as a town girl in the seventies, dreaming of being taken home on country roads. Later, as a young mother living, not in the Rocky Mountains, but in the woods of Oregon, I played his music to my small children, singing to them of "Poems and Prayers and Promises" and the happiness of "Sunshine on My Shoulders."

In June 1997, more than twenty years after seeing him perform the first time, Steve and I took our young children to hear Denver sing at the Britt Festival, at an outdoor, grassy, hillside amphitheater, where his singing filled our senses and he sang about "Leaving on a Jet Plane" and hating to go. Less than four months later, he made his final leaving, not on a jet plane, but in a Long-EZ aircraft that crashed into the Monterey Bay.

✿

Sometimes leaving on a jet plane is waylaid by circumstances out of our control. In mid-March 2015, I went to Colorado to see my friend, Christy, for what I pretty much knew would be our last visit together. That final visit, however, nearly never found its beginning.

When I got to my gate at the airport, I stepped up to the counter and said, "I still need my seat assignment."

The round, thirty-something man said, "The flight is overbooked. We don't have a seat for you. You'll have to reschedule."

"But I bought my ticket weeks ago."

"It's spring break, and all flights are overbooked," he said.

"You don't understand. I have to get on this flight. My friend is dying."

"I'm sorry," he said again. "Can I see your boarding pass?" I handed it to him and, unable to control myself, burst into tears, covering my face with my hands, my elbows on the counter, as other seat-less customers lined up behind me, each worried that he or she would also be bumped from the flight. The airline attendant then tapped away on his computer, effectively deleting me from the flight, and asked me to sign away my rights to a spot on the plane.

Sometimes, even when you try not to, making a scene in public is unavoidable. I signed the damn form because I was distraught and couldn't think properly. My normal ability to summon fighting words had left me; I was rendered mute of words but not of sound. I moved to the side counter, leaning on it, and continued to sob quietly into my hands as the airline attendant then asked for volunteers to give up their seats; the flight was overbooked by as many as six people. I had not volunteered. He had chosen for me.

I watched as the needed number of passengers gave up their seats in exchange for $400 vouchers and the gate area emptied, except for the last passenger, a young man who stepped forward and said, "She can have my seat," nodding in my direction. I don't know if he was motivated by the $400 voucher or if he was that rare, compassionate person who empathized with a distraught stranger. I didn't question it, though, just expressed my sincere thanks, boarded the plane, and arrived in Denver two hours and forty minutes later.

I spent four days with Christy. We went to her physical therapy. We went to the medical marijuana doctor. We went to the hydration center and lymphatic massage therapist. We ate lunch in Boulder at Med, her favorite Mediterranean restaurant, except I ate most of the food because she could hardly eat. We stopped at Lush to pick up the aromatherapy bath oils that helped her relax and experience fleeting moments free of pain. We hosted a get-together at her sister's house, where I was housesitting, for some members of her writing salon. We recorded Christy telling funny stories from her life. We worked in her office, sorting photographs. We walked slow, steady circles around the park half a block down the street from her house. We walked an even bigger slow and steady circle out in open space with views of the Flatirons on a day so clear you could have heard Barbra Streisand's voice flying down from the mountain tops about seeing forever. Amidst all the measured, methodical doing, we talked. And we talked. And we talked.

When it came time for me to leave, at around 9:00 p.m., Christy sat cozied in a blanket in a recliner, exhausted and ready for sleep.

"Wow, she really came alive for you," her mother had said when I first walked in four nights before. But now, after the toll of so much activity, she was ready for rest. As I said goodbye, I couldn't contain my tears. How do you say a permanent goodbye to a friend without crying?

✪

If I were to choose a symbol for leaving, it would be the monarch butterfly, all papery delicacy and queen of transformation the way they progress through four stages of metamorphosis, leaving each stage to reenter anew, from egg to larvae to pupa to butterfly. But this transformation does not signal the end of their leavings. In autumn, utilizing air currents and thermals, a kaleidoscope of monarchs can migrate up to three thousand miles one-way, travelling between fifty to a hundred miles a day, seeking protection from cold.

Eastern monarchs of North America overwinter in the same dozen forests of oyamel fir trees in the Sierra Madre Mountains of Mexico. West of the Rockies, monarchs travel from as far north as Canada to Santa Cruz and Pacific Grove along the Monterey Bay of the Pacific Ocean and further on south, down to San Diego and Baja California. This generation of monarchs is called the "super generation" for their ability to live eight times longer than their parents and grandparents and travel ten times farther. They travel by day and roost by night in clusters by the thousand, preferring the shelter of the same groves of eucalyptus, cypress, and Monterey pine year after year.

The incredible thing is that no single monarch butterfly that migrates the long distance to its overwintering grounds makes the return trip north in the spring. It takes up to four generations to complete the return trip. That means every single butterfly travels by some innate sense of purpose, guided by the sun and magnetic pull of the earth, committed to the process of travel, a steady ticking of repetition that serves a natural balance and order, an acceptance of and devotion to leaving that is hidden within their DNA.

❁

Some leavings are temporary. To migrate is the seasonal movement of leaving one locale for another and then returning. In the town where I live, I'm witness to this process of leaving as great skeins of Canada geese migrate, honking loudly as they pass overhead, flying in wedges across the sky. Gaggles of them rest in the meadows at the bottom of my road, wading in the spongy grass saturated by rainfall as they share space with the cows and horses who are never afforded the opportunity to leave. In spring, pairs of geese often split from the crowd to lay eggs at neighboring ponds and raise their young, swimming regally in the dark, cool water and shitting heaps along the ponds' edges.

Every fall, Chinook salmon migrate up Applegate River, branching off to swim up Williams Creek, then forking either east or west and on into the tributaries that diverge further up our valley. They struggle upstream toward their place of origin to spawn and die in the waters that gave them life. Their hatchlings then continue the migratory process of leaving that has occurred for as long as salmon have swum in the ocean.

What is a newer phenomenon, but no less cyclic, is the arrival of "trim-migrants" in September and October, looking for seasonal work in the marijuana industry. They arrive in droves in all manners of vehicles or by thumb on the highway. Some have connections to growers. Others sit on the bench in front of the general store or walk the road, holding cardboard signs that say: "Experienced Trimmer Looking for Work." The town swells to what seems like double its population for a few months, and then, like the rufous hummingbirds that must leave before the cold, many of these migrant workers take their earnings and disappear south to the desert or tropics.

✸

My cat, Lacey, was born a week after my twenty-second birthday, in the farmhouse bathroom, where I lived on six acres in Santa Cruz with a bunch of hippies. She was a gray, striped tabby with a white leopard belly, and the first cat I ever had.

We spent the first few months of her life migrating back and forth between Santa Cruz and southern Oregon because I had moved out of the farmhouse not long after she was born and we lived out of my truck. We camped at campgrounds. We occasionally stayed in motels. We slept in the back of my truck and in my brother's VW bus when we road-tripped with him. Sometimes she'd curl up in my lap; other times she'd drape herself over my shoulder, two front paws and head facing forward to the ongoing miles of outstretched highway.

When living on the road grew tiresome and the opportunity arose, we landed at the tiny home in Forest Knolls, California, where the land rolled in tree-lined waves and the sun crept between ridges. Steve put a thin log from the outside garden up to our bedroom window, where he had removed one of the small square panes of glass from a multitude of squares. He attached a flap of rubber converting the windowpane into a cat door. Lacey came and went as she pleased, but at night she'd burrow under the covers with me. She'd sleep curled in the crook of my elbow. Once, when she was still a kitten, she nursed on my breast, push-pawing my chest. One could say, if I were a witch, she would be my familiar. In the order of things, I have often said, Lacey was my first child. But then I became pregnant with my first human child, and Lacey and I left Forest Knolls for Oregon that Independence Day in 1989, when I got a blowout in the flat lands of Northern California and discovered myself to be not as independent as I once thought or wanted.

Other than a winter spent in northern Michigan my senior year of high school, I have only ever lived in two states: California, where I was born and raised, and Oregon, where I have spent the bulk of my adult life. In Oregon, there is great pride in being a "true Oregonian," meaning those who were born here, not transplanted from other places, especially those invaders from California. It took many years to shed the stigma of being a Californian. And while at one time, I embraced—even glorified—being from The Golden State, I have now lived in Oregon nearly a decade longer than I lived in California, and I have produced two organically grown "true Oregonians," one of whom has gone on to produce one of her own in a second generation, which feels like some sort of arrival.

This is my migration story. The freedom of my choices afforded by colonialism and white privilege. Some migrations are permanent leavings, marked by a lack of return. My own, taken willingly, has benefitted from the historical oppression of others. For the Takelma and Tututni peoples who, for thousands of years, inhabited this land I now call home, their permanent leaving was not by choice. In 1856, they were forcibly relocated to the Coast Indian Reservation, a 120-mile-long strip of land hundreds of miles away that has since been reduced into the 5.852 square mile Siletz Reservation.

❂

Some leavings rely on movement, as if passages are dependent on wings, on currents of air or currents of water, made on foot, by boat, or wheels—both mechanized and naturally turned, by plane, train, or automobile. Some leavings happen at a standstill—at a bedside or over the phone or sitting at a kitchen table, reading a long rambling letter or a short curt note or even, god forbid, a text.

❂

Sometimes a leaving happens midstream in the writing of an essay on leavings. A friend, who has been ravaged by the slow decay of multiple sclerosis for twenty-one years, leaves her worn-out body.

She is a former lover of Steve's, from years before we met, who once told me that at the time of their fledgling relationship, she wanted more than anything to have a baby with the man who would one day father my children. She went on to have children of her own, a son and a daughter, and welcomed me as a friend despite being the one left behind by my lover, once hers.

I learn of her leaving while FaceTime-ing with Steve, who is in France visiting Akela. He learned the news on Facebook. Hearing the news shocks because in that moment I am not expecting it, but it doesn't shock because every time I saw this friend, she looked frailer than the last, more narrow and angular, more bones than tissue. There is some measure of relief in her leaving. I feel sad and regretful not to have seen her one last time, but then I embrace her release from pain and suffering.

It's odd to learn of a personal friend's death through digital media, and I think about how the world is changing, how the present state of technology creates a new dynamic of interaction and communication. After talking with Steve and Akela, I get online and find the post that declares my friend's death. I scroll through the comments, a livestream of condolences and grief that multiplies as I read. I leave my own comment. Another friend "likes" it. This is the new world, a digital reality where instead of such news arriving via a phone call, it is relayed in a perpetual feed in the virtual realm and then passed on via a video chat on a screen. Fading fast are the days when neighborhood kids played together in the streets as daylight disappeared, until mothers yelled names from front-door stoops, calling their children home to dinner; a time when social interaction existed solely in either flesh, over a telephone wire, or on the physical page in handwritten letters. More and more, those who are born know nothing of this old world. In modern-day America, especially, we are leaving it behind.

Leavings are not always representative of what is gone or lost or missing. Sometimes, leavings are what remains or what gets left behind physically. Crust from too-hard bread. Scrapings of soup in a homemade ceramic bowl. Potato peelings in the sink. A sprig of parsley that garnishes salad. Lipstick on the rim of a cold, half-drunk cup of coffee. A worn, overstuffed chair that didn't fit in the back of a pickup when the last tenant moved. Scraps of silk after a dress pattern has been cut. An old coat in a free box. Burgundy and ochre leaves carpeting the ground beneath deciduous trees. Words in a concession speech, a goodbye letter, a divorce filing. The difference when one is subtracted from two.

Remnants, residue, remainders.

What does that make us? The ones who are left behind? Are we, too, the leavings?

✸

We had only been living in the school bus on our newly purchased property for two weeks when my grandfather died of a heart attack and I flew with toddler Lily to Nebraska for the funeral. Steve took this opportunity to go work in California, and we left our recently relocated cats alone, with a neighbor to check on and feed them. When we returned, only one cat remained: Minu. Lacey was nowhere to be seen, and the friend who had been left in charge of them said that almost immediately, Lacey had disappeared. This left me in a state of grievous worry that a predator had caught her.

After a week or two, Steve visited our old residence on Craig's land, where the new tenant mentioned that a cat had been hanging around for a couple of weeks, meowing at the door. Steve told him to call us the next time he saw this cat, and sure enough, it was Lacey. Lacey had migrated six miles across the valley, back to the place she knew as home. I've often wondered how she accomplished this. Did she travel by day or by night? I assume she went cross-country through meadows and forest, not by road. As she did this, what did she see? Cows? Horses? Deer, raccoons, or foxes? Did she hunt mice or birds? Did she at any time take refuge and curl under a shrub to rest, or did she make her way directly? Mostly I wonder how she navigated to the precise location. Did she rely on her sense of smell and the trajectory of the sun, or was it the flow of the creeks that guided her? Are cats like monarch butterflies? Do they have a circadian clock within their brain and within their whiskers (the way monarchs have one within their antennae), which synchronizes to determine time of day with position of the sun? Perhaps that is what orients them, like a compass aligned to magnetic or true north.

✸

Sometimes leavings happen in flocks, pods, packs, or herds. Sometimes they happen utterly alone.

Near the end of Lacey's life, I took her to the vet because she began having erratic breathing episodes. The vet took an X-ray and discovered that Lacey had a tumor on her heart. She also said that Lacey's heart was abnormally large for a cat and it was a wonder she had lived so long. But wouldn't having an abnormally large heart be precisely the reason for a lengthy and well-lived life?

When Lacey made her final leaving, I was in Portland with the family for Akela's birthday to see the 2008 US Olympic gymnastics team perform at the Rose Garden. I had asked a friend to check on our animals, and when I called her from the motel the morning after the exhibition, she said Lacey had died in the night, curled in a ball in her bed with her front paws together as in prayer. More than twenty years Lacey and I had been together, and I always thought I'd be present when she died. My friend said Lacey probably was waiting for me to leave, that I was her tether to the physical world; she needed me gone to make her departure. I want to believe this. It's better than believing she felt abandoned and died of a broken, enlarged heart.

My Grandma June left her body during the time span of a dinner. My aunts were at her bedside in the assisted care facility when she said, "I wish we had laughed more." Was there ever a more honest reflection at the end of a life than that? They didn't realize this was a clue and left to get dinner. She passed on by herself while they were out. Perhaps she preferred it that way.

My mother's best friend, Mary, was preparing tea in her kitchen. She was readying to catch a train from San Bruno to San Jose to spend the night in a hotel before early morning cataract-removal surgery. Surgery terrified her. The tea, I suppose, was meant to calm her. Perhaps it was chamomile, valerian, lemon balm, or passionflower? The doctor's office called a friend the next day saying Mary was a no-show. The friend called the hotel and learned Mary never checked in. Her phone went unanswered, so the police were called to investigate. They found her dead on the kitchen floor from a heart attack, the tea kettle burning away on high on the stove, no longer whistling as it was, by that point, empty.

For years, every time I think of Mary, the refrain that goes through my head is *Why did she have to leave me*? I feel this refrain like a throbbing ache in the joints that never finds its balm.

When I entered her apartment for the first time after her death, the thing that struck me most deeply was not the piles of belongings—the leavings—to be sorted or the lack of her gentle, kind presence. It was the white linoleum of the kitchen floor. Cold, hard, unforgiving. The place of her leaving. Alone.

❋

Sometimes the final leaving you put your whole self into turns out not to be the final one after all. Two weeks after my visit to Denver to see Christy, she managed to fly to Minneapolis, accompanied by a helpful and devoted friend, for the Association of Writers & Writing Programs conference. This was quite an endeavor for a woman on oxygen, in chronic pain, and weakened from the allopathic fight to stay alive, but she knew going to Minneapolis gave her the opportunity to see and say goodbye to many friends from all over the country, gathered simultaneously in one location. She rented a high-rise Hilton suite that had plenty of room for groups of friends to visit, and rather than exerting her limited energy on attending panels, readings, and the book fair, she mostly stayed in her room and had friends come to her.

Having the opportunity to see her again so soon after what was to be our last visit made me think the future held more visits (or at least one more), and because I had been fortunate to have just shared so many days with her one-on-one, I kept my distance somewhat, wanting to respect her space to connect with the many people who had not been as lucky as me. Was this wrong? Should I have devoted more time to her? "I thought I would see you more," she said regretfully on the phone after the conference.

On the last night in Minneapolis, Christy and I and seven of her friends from Denver met for dinner at Loring's Pasta Bar. We ate and drank and shared stories from the conference and talked writing from all angles. It was a leisurely dinner since we were in a private room, removed from the main part of the restaurant. But after a time, there were early flights to catch for some, and Christy was quite exhausted. A couple of us had walked to the restaurant from our hotels, but Christy's was too far for her to walk. Cabs were called, and suddenly the group was rushing through the restaurant to meet their drivers, with me trailing behind. Christy was escorted so quickly I barely had a chance to hug her goodbye before she was whisked into the taxi. There was no lingering moment to drink in the sight of each other, no drawn-out touch to feel the solidity, and therefore the realness, of the other, no protracted moment—*this may be the last time I will ever see you*—and thus, there were no tears.

"Bye! Love you, love you!" we yelled at each other. Doors slammed shut on the two taxis, and they brusquely pulled away from the curb.

I started walking with a friend back to our motels together. I made it barely half a block. Sometimes, after a tearless final leaving, its irrevocability crumples you to the sidewalk of a downtown Minneapolis street and you bawl like a baby.

Hans Christian Andersen said, "Where words fail, music speaks." But what of music with lyrics? The poetry of song? Ballads of the bards and druids who told oral histories while strumming a harp or lute? What of the country crooner in cowboy boots and Stetson who recounts his woes and loss? And the pop and soul divas who belt their blues in lyrics seeping with leaving? What of folk troubadour Bob Dylan, who was honored with the Nobel Prize in Literature for his words set to music?

Song lyrics often strike at the heart of leavings in a way that other words don't seem to touch us. Maybe it's the accompaniment of the music to the lyrics that spurs a sense of drama, like a movie soundtrack to our actual lives, that is what Hans Christian Andersen speaks of? But isn't it the words, the lyrics, that incite tweens to swoon as they listen to Top 40 radio, that hit us hard as we drive in the car after an unfortunate breakup, that move us to tears when played at a memorial service?

Consider this: as Dylan says "Farewell" to his own true love, he sings that it is not the leaving that is grieving him, but the fact that his darlin' will stay behind. Phil Collins warns that it's harder to come back "If Leaving Me Is Easy." When she's gone, Bill Withers bemoans there "Ain't No Sunshine." Before leaving, Crosby, Stills, and Nash ask for "Just a Song before I Go." Chicago fears losing the biggest part "If You Leave Me Now." Pink Floyd "Wish[es] You Were Here." Fleetwood Mac demands you "Go Your Own Way" while KC and the Sunshine Band pleads "Please, Don't Go." Hall & Oates laments the fact that "She's Gone" while Maria Taylor breathes a sigh of relief that she finally made a "Clean Getaway." The Who declares "I'm Free!" with unadulterated gusto. Tracy Chapman reminisces about her lover's arm wrapped round her shoulder as they speed so fast, but in the end, tells her to keep on driving in that "Fast Car." John Denver apologetically says, "Goodbye Again," wondering why they always fight when he has to go. Tom Petty isn't worried about breaking her heart; he admits to being a bad boy, overjoyed to be "Free Falling." Supertramp has no worries, up before the dawn, saying "Goodbye Stranger." After it's over, Adele is reluctantly determined to find "Someone Like You." And Eric Clapton, like so many of us, poignantly grieves about "Tears in Heaven."

Some leavings are silent. At the beginning of seventh grade, when I was transitioning from the security of elementary school, where I had attended with the same group of children from kindergarten through sixth grade, to the much larger and intensified social pressure of junior high, my best friend at the time (for hierarchies of friendships are fluid as water) abandoned me without a word. One day we were laughing hysterically in our seats at the movie theatre, watching Goldie Hawn and Chevy Chase hijack a cab in San Francisco on their way to the Opera House to prevent the assassination of the pope, and the next thing I knew: silence. She stopped talking to me. We didn't fight. There was no misunderstanding—other than the fact that I had no idea why she dropped me. She never gave any indication as to why she no longer wanted to be friends. My calls were not returned, my letters unanswered. When I saw her in the halls at school, she ignored me.

Eventually, I heard third-hand that she thought I was "prissy," a fussy, prudish girl who wouldn't take risks and didn't like to get dirty. This hurt because it was an insult, but mostly it hurt because it wasn't true. I laugh at this now because as a woman who lives off the grid, with an outhouse rather than flush toilet, who chops wood and builds fires to stay warm, who bathes outdoors year-round, prissy doesn't describe me. Not now, not then. Prissy people don't grow up to live rustic lives. What did describe me then, however, was *insecure* and *naïve*. My crime as a twelve-year-old: I didn't want things to change. I wasn't ready for the fast pace and turmoil of adolescence. I still wanted to *play*. I didn't want to leave that familiar life called childhood, yet those around me seemed to thrive on the social pressures of becoming teenagers: the demand to be fashionable, the back-stabbing gossip of cliques and race to be popular, the experimentation that comes with burgeoning sexuality. I was lost and alone, wandering the recesses of campus at lunch rather than sitting down to eat. When you're moving, it's more difficult to be identified as the loser girl who has no friends.

I think of all the leavings, the silent ones are not necessarily the most grievous, but they are the most cutting. They strip you of agency, denying the basic right of knowledge via communication. My (ex-)friend's silent leaving led me to believe there was something inherently wrong with me. At the age of twelve, it's hard to realize otherwise.

❂

Sometimes leavings are repetitive. Exact details might change, but the gist is the same. I once had a lover I tried to leave over and over. He scooped me up like a bird with a broken wing, even though he was more broken than

I was. He was a dozen years older, which wouldn't have been a problem except he arrogantly professed himself to be my "teacher" and belittled me in the process. At nineteen, I was young, but I sure as hell knew that a lovers' relationship based on such a power differential was no true or healthy relationship. We fought often, sometimes physically. And slowly my spirit dwindled. After the first year, I summoned my independence and moved out. During that second year, I was forever leaving him. Until one day I wasn't. As John Green writes in his young adult novel *Paper Towns*, "It is so hard to leave—until you leave. And then it is the easiest goddamned thing in the world."

✪

Sometimes, leavings never happen at all. They remain locked in the realm of potential, an almost leaving. And everyone involved is the better for it. A daughter survives a life-threatening illness. A husband commits to working through the challenges with his wife.

✪

When I was a little girl, no younger than five and no older than seven, my mother took me and my friend, Loli, with her to the hardware store on El Camino Real, a busy six-lane road. She parked next to the sidewalk and left us out front by the car. This was the early seventies, when parents often left their children to fend for themselves without the worry of something bad happening. My mother told us to stay put and went inside to buy whatever she needed. It wasn't long before the idea of walking to Loli's house hatched in our minds and we were leaving my mother's car behind, making our way to Loli's apartment a mile and a half away, past Town & Country Shopping Center, through an underpass below the train tracks on Embarcadero Road, then down Alma Street, another busy four-lane road that paralleled the tracks. It was a long trek on our short legs and quite the navigational feat for children so young, as we had to maneuver a complicated path of intersections. But finding my way has always come easily. It's as if I was born with an innate compass, like that of monarch butterflies, Canada geese, or cats even, one that guides me from point A to point B even if I've never travelled the in-between. When we finally arrived, my mother was there with Loli's parents, much relieved to see us.

This was my nature from the time I was a young child. I loved to explore, was fiercely independent (and often solitary), and needed no encouragement leaving the nest. At the age of sixteen, I left home and went away to boarding school by my own volition, paid for with the college fund my grandfather had left me, which I thought I'd never need because at that time, I had no intention of ever going to college. Two years later, after graduation, I returned home to my parents' house just long enough to work and save the money I needed to get an apartment with a friend in Santa Cruz.

Some birds leave the nest before they have learned to fly. Others must be nudged. Some birds nest in the ground while others nest in trees. Of my two daughters, one needed no encouragement; she chose to attend college on the opposite side of the country and then moved to France after graduation; the other has barely left home, choosing instead the comfort of our family unit and security of the property where she grew up. One of my daughters burrows, the other flies.

✺

The ancient Greek tragedian Aeschylus said, "Time brings all things to pass." According to fossil records, five mass extinctions (a die-off of at least 75 percent of species) have swept the earth. The largest mass extinction was the End-Permian—250 million years ago—where approximately 90 percent of species went extinct. Scientists debate whether or not we are currently amid the sixth wave of mass extinction. A 2019 United Nations report from a three-year study compiled by 145 experts from fifty countries (with 310 contributing authors) "finds that around 1 million animal and plant species are now threatened with extinction, many within decades, more than ever before in human history." Species are estimated to be leaving the planet at a rate of tens to hundreds of times (and accelerating) the natural "background rate" of one to five per year. The human population, on the other hand, keeps growing. In 1970, the world population was 3.7 billion. As of November 2020, it is 7.8 billion and is expected to rise to 8 billion by 2023. Humans have more than doubled in fifty years' time.

✺

Twice I have given birth, worked to exhaustion to push a tiny human from my body, felt the clamp of vice-like squeezing, the burn of the ring of fire—a sensation like I would burst and rip apart into jagged pieces—then the sudden relief when the head emerged, the slippery body of the baby slid out, left me, made us two rather than one. Maybe birth is not so much an emerging as it is a leaving. Maybe the one being born experiences it in reverse, not as a gift that is given, but as a subtraction, a taking away, leaving the one and only place we might ever experience a true sense of safety, warmth, peace, and comfort. Maybe that's why as adults we have no memory of our entry into the world. Maybe the process of leaving the womb and entering a place of sensory overload is so traumatic we have blocked it from our minds.

❋

After Lacey's death, I carried her body in the bed in which she had died into the crematorium, a stand-alone, large, aluminum shed with a concrete floor and a barrel-drum incinerator inside that the woman who owned the pet cemetery had already preheated. I had opted for a private cremation, so there would be no comingling of ashes between Lacey and another animal.

My family came with me. Before it was me and Steve—before it was me, Steve, and Lily—before it was me, Steve, Lily, and Akela—it was me and Lacey, and I was distraught over saying goodbye to my beloved cat. Lacey had been with me half my life and almost all my adult years. I needed privacy to cry and grieve. But the cemetery woman kept talking; she wouldn't shut up. At first it was polite, kind even. She said we could stay there in the shed while the cremation was happening, that we could take all the time we needed, no need to rush off. But she kept yammering on and on, looking at Lacey, touching her, commenting on the softness of her fur, commenting on her markings, talking casually about her own cat who resembled Lacey. "I had a cat who looked almost exactly like her . . ." Blah, blah, blah, blah. It was obvious Cemetery Woman's work had desensitized her. This was business as usual: dead animal comes in, put it in the incinerator, bag up the ashes, collect payment. I wanted to scream, "Shut the fuck up!" But I didn't because for one thing, I was on her property, soliciting her services, and it would be rude. But for another, all I could do was hold back the sobs that were waiting to erupt in great guttural bursts. I would never stroke Lacey again. I was committing her to fire, leaving her to burn.

Cemetery Woman picked Lacey's stiff body up out of the bed, placed her on what looked like a metal pizza spatula, and slid her body inside the incinerator the way you'd slide a pizza into an oven. She pressed a button, and the incinerator went *Whoosh* with flame. I sat for a few minutes on the one plastic chair in the building, listening to the raging furnace. My family went out to the car. When I joined them, the sky was aflame in scorching magenta. Fire within. Fire Without. No escaping it.

What is the color of leaving? I suppose if leavings have color, it depends on their temperature. Even hot and cold contain their own variations on the spectrum. Imagine a sexually charged couple pulsing with unfulfilled desire. Their hands squeeze and stroke, their breath lingers heavy and humid on lips and against necks, their pelvises press together. But for whatever reason, they are unable to fulfill their urges. Maybe it's an inappropriate place to copulate—the hallway at a friend's dinner party or the lunchroom at work. Maybe one of them is married and trying desperately (albeit poorly) to remain faithful. Maybe they believe sexual intercourse is reserved solely for the marriage union and are waiting for the ceremony. Whatever the reason, they part, alive with energy, high-pitched, like a vibrating string on a violin.

Passion is described as hot, like fire. But leavings in the throes of sexual yearnings are very different than leavings by fire. Both are hot, but one is driven by blood while the other erases it. Which shade of fire belongs to which? Fire that burns the hottest is white. Yellow flame is cooler, followed by orange, and red flame cooler still. It takes a temperature of between 1400 and 1800 degrees Fahrenheit to burn a body to ash. The sun burns at 9,941 degrees Fahrenheit and lightning at 54,032. White hot flame. The color of purification. A color that scorches clean and true. But what of the heart of those left behind? What of the pain of permanent leavings? Red is typically the color associated with love. Is the color of passionate leavings cinnabar or vermillion, scarlet or cherry? What of leavings that leave you cold? Is their color the blue of glacial ice? Or does the parting leave you feeling more like stone, slate gray, perhaps, or steel?

✪

Of all the leavings, which is worst? Is it the unexpected? The raw, stabbing, and visceral? Is it the inevitable yet sorrowful, the one so unfair as to be damnable of the universe? Or is it the one that requires—no, demands—getting used to? The common, the expected, the prepared for, the repetitive. Perhaps establishing divisions of hierarchy would be a disservice to leavings because each one exists independently from others, their depth of impact determined by the circumstances in which they happen and to whom, something that cannot be compared. For some, though, the worst leaving declares itself with absolute certainty. It steals from your subconscious as you sleep, waking you in an eruption of deep, guttural moaning so loud and animal-like you don't recognize your own voice as human.

✪

Akela stood on the porch of her new residence, a barn-red, two-story Victorian in the central Pennsylvanian town where she attended college. Only a month later she would be forced to leave this house. Maybe it was a mother's intuition of an impending crisis. Maybe it was our history of leavings that caused my flow of tears. For her it wasn't sad. She had returned to school for her senior year of college after a year studying abroad. The brightness of the future cast a gleaming light. She was all prospects and opportunity, ripe with the freedom of independence, not thinking about how the sheer gleam of possibility does not guarantee goodness, as life is wont to teach us. And as I pulled away from the curb, leaving her behind, sorrow—that old, familiar friend—gripped me from the inside, the way your breath catches when you plunge into cold water.

I drove through the rolling fields of Pennsylvania, cornstalks dry and shaved to a stubble, listening to the melancholy music of Hozier. I passed a mother sitting on the ground in an empty field, her little boy and baby in a stroller, watching the sun set into clouds painted a brilliant wash of fire and wine. This image permanently lodged in my mind. Like a highway marker, it reinforced in me the road I had taken, a time now left behind. I was once that young mother, sitting in a field with her small child and baby, gazing at a turbulent sunset. As I approached Washington, DC, an hour or two later, the darkened night sky illuminated in striking flashes of electric white gold.

ANTIDOTE TO GRIEF

Moon and Stars

We've just finished eating dinner. It's late, too late to be eating and much too late for a two-year-old to still be awake. I'm sitting at the table next to the sliding glass door. My grandson has figured out how to open the slider by pushing sideways on the glass, and he opens it. My instinct is to stop him. It's dark, and he might wander into the yard. But cool, damp air wafts in, and it feels fresh and welcome after the past three weeks of dense smoke from forest fires, which are burning all over Oregon. For weeks, our home has been surrounded by lightning-induced fires that caused the region to have the worst air quality in the world, oscillating between "very unhealthy" and "hazardous." The closest fire is the Creedence Fire, just over the mountain from us, about seven miles away. It rained two days ago, enough to temporarily clear the air, allowing us to see the mountains, which were obscured by the smoke, and to experience sunshine, clouds, and blue sky. I tell Tristan, "You can leave the door open, but stay on the porch."

He begins to walk away but returns immediately and says, "Bubby, come see moon. Ghee-Ghee, come see moon. Mommy, come see moon."

"I'll come see the moon with you," I say and walk out onto the lawn in the dark with him.

"Up, up," Tristan says, arms reaching for me. I pick him up, and he wraps his little arms around my neck.

"I don't see the moon," I say. "Maybe it hasn't come up yet. But look, you can see stars in the sky."

"Yeah," he says, in his lilting voice, half excitement, half awe, that turns up at the end, curled like a dog's tail.

He gazes upward with me. It is not one of those shockingly bright, star-filled nights. There are some clouds and still a slight haze from smoke. But we haven't seen stars for weeks, so to see the few that we do feels like finding the pot of gold at the end of a rainbow.

Tristan puts his head on my shoulder and snuggles. I squeeze his little body and sway side to side. He lifts his head again and looks up. "Look at the stars," he says.

Then he puts his hands flat on my cheeks, one on each side, cupping my face, and gives me a perfect little kiss right on the lips. It is a flawless moment, me and him, out in the dark, gazing at the stars in the fresh air. One I want to suck every ounce from, as if by osmosis I might absorb the tenderness right through my skin and into my bloodstream. Then he opens his mouth wide and slobbers all over my mouth and chin. My face is wet with toddler drool. But this isn't enough for him. He sticks out his tongue and in one long swoop licks my cheek.

Music and Dancing

"Watch some songs?" Tristan says. "Watch dancing one."

Every morning, this ritual. As soon as I'm up, drinking my coffee, iPad mini open in my lap to check emails and read the daily news, Tristan is climbing into my lap asking to "watch songs." It first started with the *Ghostbusters* theme song. That was our staple since he was four months old. We didn't watch it but listened. Once he grew into toddlerhood, we began watching music videos and added other songs to the repertoire. Fleetwood Mac's "Tusk," in which the USC marching band parades onto the stage, snare, tenor, and bass drums beating as horns, mellophones, and tubas bellow shrilly. Tristan pounds his own tom-tom drum with enthusiasm, in perfect time to the music. "Big Love," which Tristan calls "Ooh Ahh" for Lindsey Buckingham's frenzied screams that accompany the fever pitch of his guitar at the end of the song. George Ezra's "Listen to the Man," starring an endearing, scruffy-faced Sir Ian McKellan, casually dressed in white jeans, tropical shirt, and black sweater, a white fedora rimmed with a pink satin ribbon on his head, perfectly lip syncing in Ezra's deep, old-man voice.

The current favorite is Justin Timberlake's "Can't Stop the Feeling!" The version we watch has an array of everyday people—from coffee shop waitress to barber to grocer and donut maker—dancing freely, each in their own unique and uninhibited way. The beat is jaunty, and from the very first notes, Tristan starts skip-dancing, like he's riding an imaginary pony, clapping or with his arms high in the air. He twirls and hops and jumps. He strikes lunging poses. Sometimes he points his arms à la John Travolta in *Saturday Night Fever*, although he's never seen anyone do this, except possibly me. Often, he bends both knees in a squat and bounces, his hands held out in front of his chest, palms facing one another about five inches apart, his mouth forming the shape of an *O*.

We watch this music video over and over and over. "Watch dancing one," he says repeatedly throughout the day, and I usually oblige him. I always join in, and sometimes his mother and Steve (whom Tristan calls Ghee-Ghee) do too, all of us dancing and clapping to the beat with utter abandon. I never tire of the song. And I never tire of the dancing. It's infectious— the beat, the lyrics, Tristan's pure, unrivaled joy. On days when Tristan is not home, the song runs in a loop through my head. This doesn't irk me. I know one day another song will dominate his attention. For now, "Can't Stop the Feeling!" fills me with resonance and contentment because along with Tristan and Justin Timberlake, I've got the feeling deep in my bones and it won't stop.

Pushcart and Pinecones

I'm sitting at my desk in the bedroom, working on my computer. Tristan is playing with his Radio Flyer pushcart, which he has filled with large, prickly pinecones and dried oak leaves, like a squirrel's nest. Our house is essentially two main rooms. One is long and narrow—twelve by twenty-four feet. Sometimes we refer to it as a caboose. It consists of the kitchen, dining, living, and play area. With the furniture and woodstove, there is only one path Tristan can travel while pushing his cart: back and forth, back and forth in a disjointed line. The bedroom is crammed so full—king-size bed, bookshelves, plants, an armoire, dresser, file cabinet, desk and chair—that there is little room to maneuver, but he utilizes this space anyway, pushing his cart from one room to the other and back again.

When he arrives in the bedroom, he attempts to swivel my office chair around so that I face him, but I am too heavy, so I spin it myself. He extends his tanned arms up to me. I reach down and pick him up, and he lays his towhead on my shoulder and wraps his arms around me. I squeeze him tightly and say, "I love you, buddy boy." Then he squirms, so I set him on his feet. He waves at me, fingers spread wide, hand rotating in a tick-tock motion the way a pendulum on a grandfather clock swings. He says,

"Bye, Lovey," in his high-pitched, sing-song voice that breaks me in the best possible way. Tender and innocent and pure. I wave back in the same fashion and say, "Bye, Lovey," back to him. He pivots his pushcart around and pushes it back into the other room.

A minute later, he returns pushing his cart and starts the procedure all over again, a ritual he initiates nearly a dozen times: the rotation of the office chair, the extended arms, the heart-melting head on my shoulder and squeezing hug, the little wave, and best of all, the "Bye, Lovey" in that precious little voice I want to bottle like a genie and call upon whenever I need magic and to make wishes I believe have the capacity to come true. One day, maybe this need to capture and contain abstractions such as his voice will wane. On that day, I will lift the bottle from the shelf where it is gathering dust, and rather than rub it to satisfy my own desire, I will toss it into the ocean, watch it drift away, a message tucked safely inside for someone else to find.

AFTERWORD

Four months after completing the manuscript of *All the Leavings*, which I began submitting to publishers in the fall of 2017, my husband, Steve, was diagnosed with stage IV liver cancer. He died seven weeks later on a Thursday morning in early April 2018.

The fact that I had written a book titled *All the Leavings*, which chronicles many of the losses I have experienced, felt like the universe had played a morbid cosmic joke on me. How could I send a book out into the world titled *All the Leavings* when it had certainly not been all the leavings?

I was left with a quandary: do I revise the manuscript to include Steve's death as the final and worst leaving of all? My instinct said no. I had already written a book that felt complete. A book in which Steve was an important supporting character, but he and our marriage were not the primary focus. To incorporate the fullness of our nearly thirty-two-year relationship would produce a far longer book than was allowable, and I did not want to tack on his death as simply another leaving; that would both be a disservice to our marriage and detract from the other narrative threads. I had to ask myself, is not including Steve's death while continuing to title the collection *All the Leavings* being dishonest to the reader? I decided it was not. The book has a starting point and an ending point, both of which are decidedly not the very beginning of my life nor the end. To write an essay collection or memoir is to choose what themes to explore and what scenes to include. It is not the same as writing an autobiography. As Judith Barrington puts it succinctly in her book *Writing the Memoir*: "An autobiography is the story *of a life:* the name implies that the writer will somehow attempt to capture all the essential elements of that life . . . Memoir, on the other hand, is a story *from a life*. It makes no pretense of replicating a whole life" (22–23). With this as a guiding principle, it felt right to not include Steve's death. What didn't feel right, however, was for you, the reader (with the exception of those who know me), to finish reading this book and not have any notion of his death or for me to not acknowledge it.

What I have come to realize going through this process and in my ruminations on leavings is that life is not static; there can never be a place or time when all the leavings have come to pass. The nature of leavings is constant. And at the end of writing a book on leavings, the worst leaving had yet to come.

Williams, Oregon
November 2020

ACKNOWLEDGMENTS

Thank you to the editors at the following publications where these essays initially appeared, some with slight variations:

"Searching for Gwen," *The Rumpus*, September 7, 2021; *A Harp in the Stars: An Anthology of Lyric Essays*, edited by Randon Billings Noble, University of Nebraska Press, October 2021

"Solving My Way to Grandma," *The Shell Game: Writers Play with Borrowed Forms*, edited by Kim Adrian, University of Nebraska Press, April 2018

"Bad Blood," *Chautauqua*, "Privacy and Secrets" issue, June 2015

"Rebound Tenderness," *The Manifest-Station*, May 12, 2015

"The Polarity of Incongruities," *r.kv.r.y quarterly*, Winter 2015, vol. xii. no. 1

"Crack My Heart Wide Open," *The Rumpus*, October 9, 2014

"Her Body, a Wilderness," *Prime Number Magazine*, Issue 61, Fall 2014

"Sojourns with Big Cats in Triptych," *Animal: A Beast of a Literary Magazine*, July 2014

"Something to Do with Baldness," *Under the Gum Tree*, January 2014

"I Have to Tell You," under the title "I Have to Tell You Something," *Hippocampus Magazine*, June 2013

"Relics" under the title "Death Box," *Connotation Press: An Online Artifact*, January 2013

Thank you to Kim Hogeland for believing in and acquiring this book, Micki Reaman for brilliant editing, and everyone at Oregon State University Press for seeing it through to publication. I am so grateful.

Thank you to my advisors at Vermont College of Fine Arts: Robin Hemley, Robert Vivian, and Sue Silverman, who has remained an ardent supporter these many years, always willing to answer questions and offer generous guidance. And to Richard McCann, who sadly left us before this book was published, I wish you were here to witness the final product. Your incisive feedback on these essays and writing wisdom has had a profound impact on me and this book.

Thank you to the Vermont Studio Center for the generous gifts of both a grant and a fellowship consecutively, which allowed for a solid portion of the writing of this book. VSC in October remains one of my most favorite places on earth.

To my literary loves, Jericho Parms and Emily Arnason Casey, thank you for your editorial insights, never-ending support, encouragement, inspiration, and your friendship. I couldn't have done it without you.

To Melissa Matthewson, I'm so thankful for your presence in my life, my sole Southern Oregon essayist/writer friend! Here's to many more long talks, both literary and personal.

Thank you to Suzanne Farrell Smith for your generosity of time to read, your brilliant thoughts and edits, and your friendship. Thank you to Alice Anderson for your exceptional manuscript review, precise edits, and positive feedback. Thank you to Sonja Livingston for your detailed peer review, suggestions, and recommendation of publication to Oregon State University Press. And to Pamela Benham Cooper, thank you for the support of time to write in a comfortable place with delicious meals, walks on the beach, glasses of prosecco, and friendship.

This book has been more than a decade in the making. In such a time span, many people have had an impact on me as a writer and this work in particular. I'd like to thank Dr. Tom Nash and Dr. Bill Gholson, whose brilliant instruction was foundational in my development as a writer, both by widening my knowledge and perspective and getting me to take myself seriously as a writer. For feedback on these essays, I'd like to thank Annie Penfield, Sheila Stuewe, Lia Woodall, Chelsea Biondolillo, Daisy Abreu, Hollie Box, Maud Macrory Powell, Sarah Braud, Melissa Bank, and Brenda Miller's postgraduate workshop at Vermont College of Fine Arts.

To my girls, Lily and Akela, I know it's probably not easy having a writer for a mother, but trust me, you will live through this! Thank you for being tolerant. I love you both so much. You mean everything to me.

And to Steve, no longer here, but no less appreciated, for the support you gave in pursuit of my writing life and your willingness for me to be a truth teller. I love and miss you. Always.

NOTES AND SOURCES

This book's epigraph is from the poem "XIX" by Dulce Maria Loynaz,
   in *Absolute Solitude: Selected Poems*, translated by James O'Connor
   (Brooklyn, NY: Archipelago Books, 2016).

"Her Body, a Wilderness"
9–10: KalmiopsisWild, "The Biscuit Fire: Time to Bury the Myth." https://
   kalmiopsiswild.org/1019/the-biscuit-fire-time-to-bury-the-myths.
9–10: United States Department of Agriculture Forest Service,
   "Kalmiopsis Wilderness, After the 2002 Biscuit Fire." https://www.
   fs.usda.gov/detail/rogue-siskiyou/recreation/?cid=stelprdb5305646.

"Relics"
27: Quoted material is from Susan Seddon Boulet, *Animal Spirits
   Knowledge Cards: Paintings by Susan Seddon Boulet* (Portland, OR:
   Pomegranate, 2007).

"I Have to Tell You"
44: The epigraph is from William Shakespeare, *Antony and Cleopatra*, Act
   II, sc. 5.

"Crack My Heart Wide Open"
65: American Foundation for Suicide Prevention, "Suicide Facts
   & Figures: United States 2020." https://www.datocms-assets.
   com/12810/1587128056-usfactsfiguresflyer-2.pdf.

"Searching for Gwen"

Additional hidden words embedded in the puzzle: essay, home, life, love, lyric, memoir, nonfiction, ode, poetry, prose.

73–74; 75–76: *Frontline* and the *Oregonian, The Meth Epidemic*, Frontline. https://www.pbs.org/wgbh/pages/frontline/meth.

73–74; 75–76: National Institute on Drug Abuse, "Methamphetamine Research Report." https://www.drugabuse.gov/publications/research-reports/methamphetamine/overview.

77–78: National Alliance of Advocates for Buprenorphine Treatment, "Substance Use Disorders: A Guide to the Use of Language." https://www.naabt.org/documents/Languageofaddictionmedicine.pdf.

"Bad Blood"

86–87: Willis C. Maddrey and Eugene R. Schiff, *The Hepatitis Workbook: A Guide to Living with Chronic Hepatitis B and C* (Schering Hepatitis Innovations, 2001).

87: Siavash Jafari, Ray Copes, Souzan Baharlou, Mahyar Etminan, and Jane Buxton, "Tattooing and the Risk of Transmission of Hepatitis C: A Systematic Review and Meta-analysis," *International Journal of Infectious Diseases* 14 (August 3, 2010): e928-e940. https://doi.org/10.1016/j.ijid.2010.03.019.

88, 91: HISTORY, "History of AIDS." https://www.history.com/topics/1980s/history-of-aids.

88: Carmen Vandelli, MD; Francesco Renzo, MD; Luisa Romanò, Ph.D.; Sergio Tisminetzky, MD; Marisa De Palma, MD; Tommaso Stroffolini, MD; Ezio Ventura, M.; and Alessandro Zanetti, PhD, "Lack of Evidence of Sexual Transmission of Hepatitis C among Monogamous Couples: Results of a 10-year Prospective Follow-up Study," *American Journal of Gastroenterology* 99:5 (May 2004). DOI: 10.1111/j.1572-0241.2004.04150.x

89: Donald G. McNeil Jr., "Precursor to HIV Was in Monkeys for Millenniums," *New York Times* (September 16, 2010). https://www.nytimes.com/2010/09/17/health/17aids.html

90: Laurel Kelly, "Consumer Health: What Is Sepsis?" Mayo Clinic, September 27, 2019. https://newsnetwork.mayoclinic.org/discussion/consumer-health-what-is-sepsis.

90: "Sepsis," United States Centers for Disease Control and Prevention. https://www.cdc.gov/sepsis/index.html.

90: "What Is Sepsis, What It Is and What It Isn't," Sepsis.org, Sepsis Alliance. December 14, 2018. https://www.sepsis.org/news/what-is-sepsis-what-it-is-and-what-it-isnt/

92–93: REBETRON™ Combination Therapy Product Information, Food and Drug Administration. https://www.accessdata.fda.gov/drugsatfda_docs/label/2002/20903s23lbl.pdf.

95–96: "Viral Hepatitis," United States Centers for Disease Control and Prevention. https://www.cdc.gov/hepatitis/hcv/index.htm.

"Rebound Tenderness"

106: Quoted material is from Louise Erdrich, *La Rose: A Novel* (New York: Harper, 2016).

"Solving My Way to Grandma"

125: "Expect the <u>unexpected</u>": "To expect the unexpected shows a thoroughly modern intellect," Oscar Wilde, *An Ideal Husband*.

126: "The first step towards change is awareness. The second step is <u>acceptance</u>": Canadian-American psychotherapist and writer Nathaniel Branden.

127: "The only thing we have to <u>fear</u> is <u>fear</u> itself": President Franklin D. Roosevelt, inaugural address, March 4, 1933.

128: "<u>Wisdom</u> is the daughter of experience": Leonardo da Vinci, *Thoughts on Art and Life*

129: "Beauty is <u>truth</u>, <u>truth</u> beauty": John Keats, "Ode on a Grecian Urn," first published anonymously in *Annals of the Fine Arts*, 1819.

"All the Leavings"

134: The epigraph is quoted from George Eliot, the pen name for Mary Ann Evans, English Victorian novelist of *Middlemarch*.

138: "Monarch Butterfly Migration and Overwintering," US Forest Service, United States Department of Agriculture. https://www.fs.fed.us/wildflowers/pollinators/Monarch_Butterfly/migration/

148: John P. Rafferty, "Biodiversity Loss," Britannica. https://www.britannica.com/science/biodiversity-loss

148: "UN Report: Nature's Dangerous Decline 'Unprecedented'; Species Extinction Rates 'Accelerating,'" United Nations. https://www.un.org/sustainabledevelopment/blog/2019/05/nature-decline-unprecedented-report.

148: "Current World Population," Worldometer. https://www.worldome-ters.info/world-population/

148: Max Roser, Hannah Ritchie, and Esteban Ortiz-Ospina, "World Population Growth," OurWorldinData.org, May 2019. https://our-worldindata.org/world-population-growth